HOW TO RETIRE EARLY
WITH LOW SAVINGS

HOW TO RETIRE EARLY

Learn strategies to generate high monthly income with low risk

Copyright © 2022 by Tarun Shah

All rights reserved. No part of this book may be reproduced or transmitted in any form or by any means, electronic or mechanical, including photocopying, recording, or by any information storage and retrieval system, without permission in writing from the publisher.

Printed in the United States of America.

HOW TO RETIRE EARLY
WITH LOW SAVINGS

LEARN STRATEGIES TO GENERATE HIGH
MONTHLY INCOME WITH LOW RISK

TARUN SHAH

DISCLAIMER

The information in this book is provided for educational and informational purposes only without any implied or expressed warranties of any kind and does not contain any financial advice. This includes any warranties of completeness, accuracy, or fitness for any purpose. The information contained in this book does not constitute nor does it intend to be investment advice, financial advice, trading advice, tax advice, professional advice, or any other advice. The ideas and strategies that I provide are general in nature and are not specific to you or anyone else. You should not make any decisions based on any of the information that is present throughout this book without first consulting a financial advisor, broker, or tax professional. In addition, I authored this book myself, and the information in it expresses my own opinions. I have no business relationship with any company whose stock is mentioned in this article, and they are not compensating me in any way.

CONTENTS

CHAPTER 1: *Introduction* — 1

CHAPTER 2: *What Psychologists Say Make Retirees Truly Happy* — 9

CHAPTER 3: *How Much Monthly Income Do You Really Need?* — 21

CHAPTER 4: *Your Options if You Have not Saved Enough* — 35

CHAPTER 5: *The Dilemma Facing Retirees Today (Low Savings, Low Returns)* — 53

CHAPTER 6: *Structure of the Next Chapters (High Income Strategies)* — 57

CHAPTER 7: *Basic Financial Terms to Understand* — 59

CHAPTER 8: *The Bucket Strategy and Why It is Important* — 73

CHAPTER 9: *Available High-Income Investments (With Pros/Cons of Each)* — 79

CHAPTER 10: *Best Investments for Early Retirement (incl. #1 Pick)* — 89

CHAPTER 11: *Strategy 1: An Early-Retirement "Set-it-and-Forget-it" Strategy* — 97

CHAPTER 12: *Strategy 2: An Active Strategy for Even Higher Returns* — 101

CHAPTER 13: *Conclusion + BONUS* — 105

CHAPTER 1
Introduction

How much do you need to retire? $500,000? $1 million?

That is the wrong question. The right question is: how much monthly **income** can my savings **generate?**

To retire early with low savings, you need to generate high monthly income on smaller savings. You cannot touch the principal as you will need to live off the interest income – for many years.

This is especially difficult to do in today's market environment. *The stock market is at all time highs with a risk of a large correction looming and the bond market is at all-time lows paying only 1%.*

As a financial veteran specializing in algorithmic trading and fixed income investments, I have tested hundreds of strategies (in both bull and bear markets) to find investments that generate high monthly income with low risk.

Unfortunately, very few investments make the cut. I will show you all the available options, provide pros and cons for each, and recommend my top pick for high monthly income, with low risk, low fees - for a set-it-and-forget-it retirement strategy.

To live a financially stress-free retirement, you will need to focus on two factors:

1. Maximize your monthly income while reducing risk.
2. Minimize your monthly expenses.

1. Maximize Your Monthly Income while Reducing Risk

It is not about how much money you have saved but how much monthly income your savings can generate.

For example, if you have a $1,000,000 portfolio and invest in safe bonds (paying 1% today), you will only generate ~$880/month. Hardly enough to live on.

However, if you have $500,000 saved and can generate 8% per year <u>safely</u>, that is ~$3,400/month. This makes retirement a possibility.

This is what the book is about and what I will show you how to do.

2. Minimize Your Monthly Expenses

Payoff your car, have zero debt, live in a cheaper state, and stay healthy. Experts agree that the number one factor for a stress-free retirement is becoming debt-free.

Studies have shown that retirees with low income and no debt were happier than retirees with high income and some debt.

> **To summarize:** early retirement on low savings is possible, but you must be laser-focused on maximizing your monthly income (with low risk) - while minimizing your monthly expenses.

What you will learn by the end of this book:

- How to invest for high monthly income while reducing risk.
- Which high-income investments to avoid and why?
- A NEW simple set it and forget it investment that provides high monthly income + downside protection + growth + low fees, perfect for retirees with low savings.
- An active investment strategy for even higher returns.

Follow the steps I outline in the book – and you can retire sooner than you think.

How the Book is Structured

The "crux" of the financial (high monthly income – low-risk strategies) starts in Chapter 5. However, I recommend reading Chapters 1-4 to understand the psychology behind a happy retirement and learn "little-known" strategies to reduce expenses and debt.

If you want to skip straight to the high monthly income strategies, I recommend starting with Chapter 5.

Towards the end of the book, I also disclose my favorite NEW investment paying *high income + downside protection + growth + low fees + paying monthly*, making it perfect for a set it and forget it early retirement strategy.

ABOUT ME

I am a veteran in the financial industry for 20+ years and have been singularly focused on monthly income strategies for retirement.

I have tested several strategies in both bull (up) and bear (down) markets to find ones that work.

The strategies I describe are through years of research and the same ones I use in my portfolio. I do not get compensated in any way for the recommendations I make. I recommend them because of their performance.

My goal is to educate you to avoid a lot of the expensive mistakes made.

Though my background is in finance, I outlined each chapter so that your level of financial expertise does not come into play. The book is designed to get the best experience from reading the chapters in order.

When it is all said and done, you will be equipped with the knowledge and strategies to get you on your way to early retirement or a financially stress-free one.

Below is how the book is structured - with the financial strategies starting in Chapter 5.

Chapter 2: What psychologists say make retirees truly happy

I detail out research performed by psychologists on what makes retirees truly happy. Although money is necessary, it is not the most important ingredient of a happy retirement.

Chapter 3: How much monthly income do you need?

Everyone's situation is different. I show you some quick and easy calculations you can make - to understand how much monthly income you will need in retirement.

Chapter 4: What can you do if you have not saved enough for retirement?

All is not lost if you have not saved enough for retirement. The vast majority of Americans have not. We show you innovative strategies to apply.

Start of the Financial Strategies

Chapter 5: The income dilemma facing retirees today

Given today's market conditions, it is more challenging than ever to generate a high monthly income with low risk. We explain the problem - so that you can understand the solution.

Chapter 6: Structure of the Next Chapters (Financial Strategies Explained)

This chapter explains how the upcoming strategy chapters are structured so you can follow along easily.

Chapter 7: Basic Financial Terms to Understand

Some basic financial terms you need to understand.

Chapter 8: The Bucket Strategy

The bucket strategy – what it is and why it is important.

Chapter 9: Current High-Income Options

I explain current high-income options available to investors and detail the pros and cons of each.

Chapter 10: My Top 4 Investments for High Monthly Income with Low Risk

I share my top four investments for high monthly income with low risk. I advise on when to use which of the investments.

Chapter 11: Strategy 1 - A Simple "Set it and Forget it" High Monthly Income Strategy.

I detail a simple strategy for a set it and forget it high monthly income strategy.

Chapter 12: Strategy 2 – Active Income Strategy for even Higher Returns

An active strategy I use for my portfolio is to generate higher returns than strategy 1. It is also simple to implement.

Conclusion + Bonus.

I summarize all the key points in the book and outline the steps to get you started too early retirement. I also reveal a bonus to book purchasers ($200 value – as a thank you!).

CHAPTER 2
What Psychologists Say Make Retirees Truly Happy

What you will learn:

1. The most critical factors to a happy retirement.
2. The resources to help you get there.

Source: verywell.com

We live in a world where pensions are rare and social security benefits are dwindling.

401(k)s are now ubiquitous with employers and have placed the burden of saving for retirement on employees. The risk that comes with investing is now shifted from employers to employees.

Most employees with access will contribute as much as possible to get ahead with retirement planning. What is concerning is that not everyone participates in retirement savings.

While 55% of non-retirees have a 401(k) or 403(b) retirement plan, those with no retirement savings amount to 25%.

However, the lack of a steady income stream is not the sole factor that fuels an unhappy retirement. Yes, financial security plays a significant role in paying for needs and wants, but it does not address the socioeconomic aspects of retirement. In addition, remember that you will no longer be part of the workforce once you quit your job.

What does this translate to exactly?

- You will no longer be part of a team or company.
- You will struggle with a loss of identity – especially after working a long time.
- You may start becoming socially isolated if you do not consciously work at it.

All these changes that come with retirement are often ignored, and retirees are ill-prepared for the decision to finally throw in the towel. Although, on the surface, this may look like the whole point of retirement, you will soon find out there is more that contributes to a happy retirement than just money.

Be Deliberate about Being Active

It is easy to sleep in, watch TV, eat and become a lazy person in retirement. There is no deadline and nowhere you need to be. Because of this, some spiral downward into an unhealthy and lonely retirement.

Per psychologists, you must be deliberate about living an active lifestyle as it impacts the quality of life in retirement.

Being physically active plays a vital role in keeping you healthy. Find a sport or physical activity that interests you, nurture it, then develop it into a hobby. There are plenty of exercises and activities that are not taxing on the body, such as swimming, golfing, biking, yoga, or simply walking. The goal is to keep your body in motion because not only is it good to exercise, but it will also prolong your life while you enjoy doing it.

Join clubs and memberships that incorporate physical activities that foster social connections (golf, tennis, pickle ball).

Figure 1: Keeping an Active Life Is Important

Plan for Healthcare

A crucial part of retiring includes planning for healthcare. Your retirement funds should cover your prescription expenses, anticipated medical bills, and emergencies.

These should all be factored in the retirement income planning.

Aside from the money, you need to ensure proximity to emergency care. Sure, you may have enough money to cover any health issue, but what good is your money if there is not a hospital nearby in times of emergency?

That house you saved up for up in the mountains may have a fantastic view, but how long would it take to get to a hospital?

Even though telehealth has become a staple these days, in-person medical care remains critical in the cases of "what if." Preexisting conditions such as high blood pressure or problems with your hip will require specialists nearby.

- Does your place of retirement have the specialists you need nearby?
- Do you have enough of them around to function as backup?
- How likely will you be utilizing their services?

As you mature throughout your golden years, these questions will become more critical, especially as aging takes a toll on your body.

Relationships And Social Interactions Matter

People are naturally social, whether you think otherwise or not.

The COVID-19 pandemic reminded us that people living in isolation do not fare well, especially when physical interactions and communications are limited.

Countless research studies show that loneliness during retirement is real and prevalent. Although everyone's pursuits of happiness are not equal, there is abundant evidence that social relationships are an enormous contributor to human well-being and happiness.

Do you currently have or are at risk of health-related conditions such as high blood pressure, depression, stress, or high body mass index (BMI)?

The Centers for Disease Control and Prevention (CDC) stated that social isolation significantly increased the risk of dying early. This risk is close to or on par with those who live a sedentary lifestyle, are obese, or smoke daily.

- The risk of dementia increased by 50% with those that are socially isolated.
- The risk of heart disease increased by 29%, stemming from a lack of social relationships.
- The risk of stroke increased by 32% due to loneliness and isolation.
- Loneliness is strongly associated with higher rates of anxiety, stress, depression, and suicide.

It is well known that physically communicating with others has positive effects on your physical and mental health.

Researchers suggest that humans are born with compassion, and this innate characteristic helps us mature as a species. Language has evolved from the need for advancing communication, and through this personal connection, compassion and empathy are nurtured.

Now that you will not see your co-workers every day make a conscious effort to find new friends and interact with others.

Join tour groups, charities for your favorite cause, or volunteer to help at a social event. There are plenty of options out there, and it would be best to fill in that social interaction void as soon as you can.

When it comes to settling down in a new place of residence, make sure to get acclimated with your neighbors before committing to settle on a deal.

Importantly, factor in your lifestyle, hobbies, religion, and political views when screening for new friends. Understand where you stand and where they stand, then figure out if you are compatible.

Do you have strong feelings on specific topics, or are you laid back and not letting these things shape you? How will your neighbors feel about your stances? Your new home will potentially be the last place you reside in, so you will need to make sure you get along with your neighbors and ensure that your interests are similar.

Set Goals to Hone Your Perspective

Figure 2: Do You Plan on Traveling?

How do you view retirement? Are you excited about the adventures that lie ahead? Can't you wait to travel the world? Or are you scared of the worst and have a negative perspective of retirement? As with any endeavor, it is essential to set your mind right so that you are in it to win it. Visualizing a fun time, success in a business deal, or acing an exam feeds positive signals to your mind and body, which sets you on a path for a good time.

Emotions carry weight when we do activities, and they can certainly work for you or against you, which applies when transitioning into retirement.

Indeed, people are different, and their emotions towards retirement may not be obvious. Therefore, it helps to write down what you think your retirement will look like. Make a list of what you want to achieve during your retirement.

- Do you want to travel the world?
- Would it be through a series of road trips, by plane, or by boat?
- What about teeing up at the most scenic golf courses around the world?

Write all your goals down and plan for them. Looking forward to and planning for your goals can work wonders to help to boost your morale and contribute to overall happiness.

It was not apparent when you were in the workforce, but you were part of a team. Goals were handed to you in the form of tasks, assignments, and projects.

The reason you made it through fifty-plus years of blood, sweat, and tears was that you had goals – goals that were subconsciously driving you through to completion and success in every situation.

When you are retired, you will need to replace your work goals with those you define. However, this can be intimidating because this may be the first time you have set your priorities but do not worry.

Have fun with it because there is no right or wrong answer here. You are your boss now, and you are planning your retirement and shaping your happiness.

Find Your Purpose

So, you were an accountant, project manager, or customer support representative, but you are now retired or looking to retire soon.

You no longer have a job to do, and that can be either good or bad. Without someone there telling you what to do, you are now on your own, which can be intimidating. The goal is to find out your new purpose during your retirement.

Studies have repeatedly shown that having a sense of purpose in life helps you live longer. The Cato 2019 Welfare, Work, and Wealth National Survey investigated those that find greater purpose and meaning in their lives.

The survey results revealed that:

- Seventy-four percent of the people believe that hard work is a reward in and of itself.
- Sixty-eight percent believe they possess personal agency (i.e., capability to originate/direct actions).
- Sixty percent value personal responsibility.

The data paints a picture of a person most likely to find purpose and meaning in their lives.

Those that value responsibility and challenging work focus on what they can control and handle rather than what is out of reach.

It leads to being more compassionate and lends well to helping to resist the urge to put people down and to feel resentment or envy of others.

What can you do to develop your sense of purpose? Remember what you did before you retired? You had a title, a job, and a purpose. However, you are now your own company. So, think about what you can produce to offer others.

Would you like to help others by giving lessons on being a better writer or speaker?

What about becoming a life or spiritual coach? Counseling or consulting on the side could help establish a sense of purpose. Your knowledge and experience are vast, and people will pay to know what you know. Put your experiences to work and develop that sense of purpose because we all have one. It is just a matter of finding out what it is and nurturing it.

Resources

Below are resources (ref. Table 1) that you can turn to to help with guidance on your retirement journey. All these resources are there for you to explore, but I recommend you pick at least one from each category and incorporate it into your retirement planning and goals. A holistic approach is best to establish a happy retirement baseline.

Table 1: Resources to Help Guide Through Retirement

Category	Resources	Website
Health	Mayo Clinic	Mayoclinic.org
	AARP	Aarp.org
	NIH Senior Health	Nihseniorhealth.gov
	Retirement Life Matters	Retirementlifematters.com
	Assisted Living Directory	Assisted-living-directory.com
Relationships	Volunteer Match	Volunteermatch.org
	Ameri Corps	AmeriCorps.org
	Elder Treks	ElderTreks.com
	Peace Corps	PeaceCorps.gov
	Retirement monthly income	Retirementmonthlyincome.com/communities
Goals	Senior Planet	Seniorplanet.org
	Interlochen Center for the Arts Adult Band Camp	Interlochen.org
	The Culinary Institute of America Boot Camps	Ciafoodies.com
	Road Scholar	Roadscholar.org
	Evergreen Club	Evergreenclub.com
Purpose	Fiverr	Fiverr.com
	Upwork	Upwork.com
	Freelancer	Freelancer.com
	Retired Brains	Retiredbrains.com

Key Points:

- Money is not the only contributor to retirement happiness.
- Be deliberate about your health, relationships, goals, and create a sense of purpose based on your interests.

Next Chapter:

Gone are the days where pension plans were the norm, and your employer did all the investing for you. These days, you are now fully responsible for planning and investing in your future.

However, how much income do you *really* need in retirement?

CHAPTER 3
How Much Monthly Income Do You *Really* Need?

What you will learn:

1. How to calculate your *ideal* monthly retirement income.
2. How to calculate *actual* monthly income and calculate the surplus/shortfall.
3. Best calculators to use.

Having a clear understanding of how much income you *need* vs. how much you will *generate* in retirement is critical.

There are many ways to reduce any shortfall, but understanding your numbers is a crucial first step.

Step 1: Calculate your ideal monthly retirement income.

How much do you need to retire happily? $500,000? $1 million?

What is the cost of maintaining your house? Your healthcare? Your food?

Just because you retire does not mean you should stop getting a regular paycheck. You still need money to live, and the only thing that's changing is your incoming requirements.

Experts agree that having a retirement income of 80% - 85% of your last salary is ideal. However, this is easier said than done. Most retirees are nowhere close to achieving this number.

However - let us stick with the general rule for now.

Aim for 80% of your pre-retirement income as your goal.

It should cover all your needs because the 20% we subtracted from the picture comes from job-related expenses that are no longer necessary.

For example, if your last salary was $100,000 a year, shoot for an $80,000 yearly income to maintain your lifestyle; this comes out to $6600 a month.

Of course, you will need to adjust this lower or higher based on what you want to do during your retirement.

Some plan for a retirement full of travel and adventures, so airfare and hotel bookings must be carefully planned. An increase in spending habits is expected in this scenario, so the 80% rule may very well be insufficient for their needs.

Other retirees will choose to live a more frugal life, a life that does not involve extravagant spending or indulging in fine dining.

A decrease in spending habits, one that's below 80% of the last salary, is often seen here.

Step 2: Calculate actual monthly income vs. expenses.

We calculated that your ideal monthly income in retirement needs to be $6600/month in the first step.

The next step is to develop a monthly expense plan.

Look at the table below to understand what a monthly expense list may look like. Note: These are hypothetical figures.

Table 2: Monthly Expenses Example in Retirement

Expense	Cost
Housing-related expenses	$2,500
Utilities	$200
Wireless phone	$100
Internet & Cable	$100
Groceries & Dining Out	$400
Auto related expenses	$600
Healthcare	$600
Entertainment	$200
Travel	$600
Misc + Savings.	$1300
Total	$6,600

> Now calculate how much monthly income you can generate in retirement to quantify the shortfall.

Figure out what your income will look like when you retire. The three primary sources are social security benefits, defined-benefit pension plans, and retirement savings. Table 3 shows an example of what a monthly income for a retiree would look like.

Table 3: Monthly Income Generation Example in Retirement

Income Source	Sum
Social security	$ 2,200
Pension	$ 800
Withdrawals from retirement savings	$ 2,500
Total	$ 5,500

Here, the monthly income you will generate is $5,500. It is a summation of the three income sources. Notice that this is below your required monthly expenses.

Here is a simple formula to calculate where you stand with respect to monthly income:

Monthly income surplus or deficiency = (Monthly Income Generated) – (Estimated Monthly Expenses)

A positive number means your income is more than expenses – good

A negative number means your income is less than expenses – needs work

Let's plug in the numbers:

Monthly income surplus/deficiency = ($5,500) – ($6,600)

Monthly Income Deficiency = ($1,100)

So, what does this $1,100 deficiency mean exactly?

It means that to live a life based on the required $6,600, an additional income of $1,100 is needed. Because the social security and pension checks are fixed, your withdrawals or returns from your retirement savings will need to increase or decrease as needed to make up for any needed difference.

In addition, if you plan on retiring early, you cannot rely on social security or a pension until later.

Your rate of return on your retirement savings, therefore, becomes critical.

> *How should you then withdraw money from your retirement savings without running out of money?*

The 4% Rule Recommended Today

4% is what advisors recommend you withdraw on your first retirement year to stay relatively safe throughout the rest of your years. Using the $2,500 monthly retirement income source as an example, you would need a total of $750,000 in retirement savings to provide a $30,000 yearly income.

Here is the simple formula for calculating retirement savings target:

Retirement savings target = Yearly income required x 25

Let's plug in the numbers:

Retirement savings target = $30,000 x 25

Retirement savings target = $750,000

These numbers are unattainable to most retirees, as they may not have such a large sum (like $750,000 saved).

The good news is that there are better options, as I will show you in subsequent chapters.

Utilize Online Retirement Calculators

Online retirement calculators are great tools to vet your numbers, as shown in the previous sections. Having accurate numbers is critical to retiring successfully.

I have reviewed several online retirement calculators, but none was as thorough and accurate as the AARP Retirement Calculator. It is free to use, and the user interface is friendly and understandable for anyone. A series of questions will be asked along the way to help guide you through the process.

Figures: 3.1 through 3.3 show screenshots of the AARP Retirement Calculator; you can see that they ask for pertinent information such as age, information about your partner, salary, and savings.

Figure 3.1: AARP Retirement Calculator Questions – Step 1a

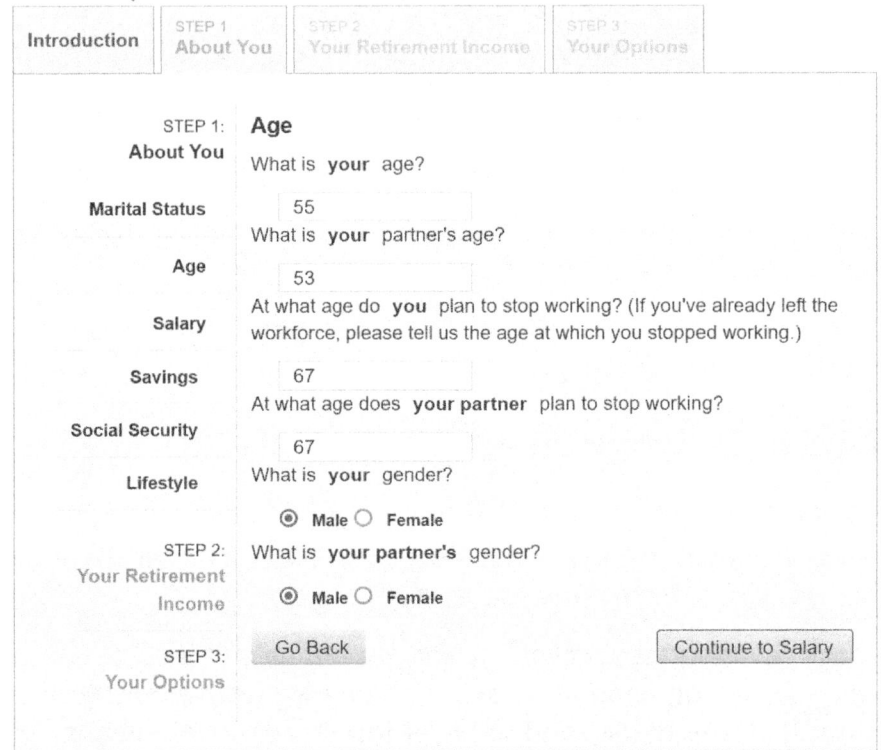

Source: AARP Retirement Calculator

Figure 3.2: AARP Retirement Calculator Questions – Step 1b

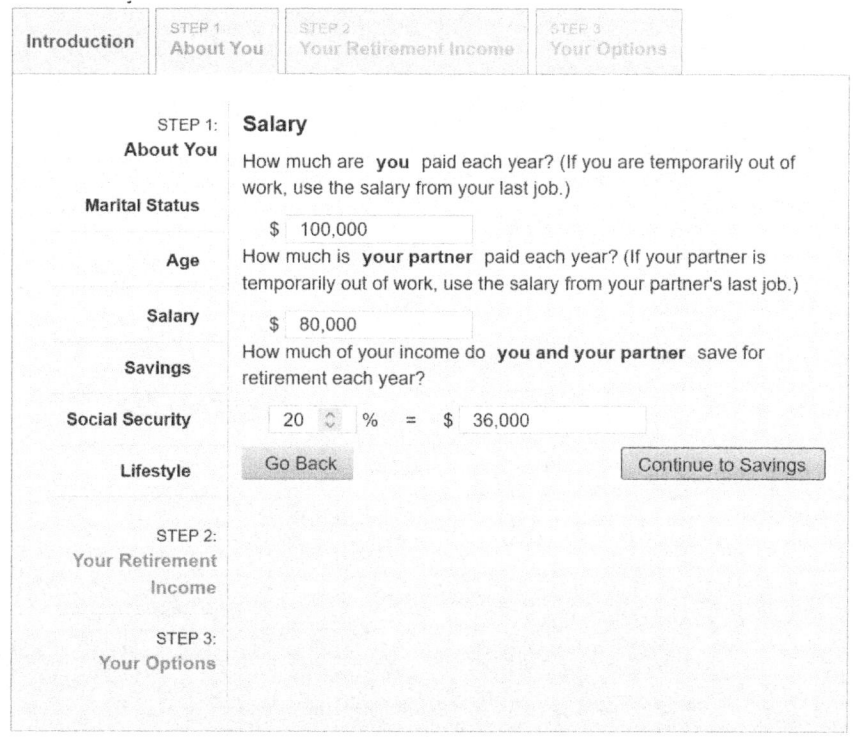

Source: AARP Retirement Calculator

Figure 3.3: AARP Retirement Calculator Questions – Step 1c

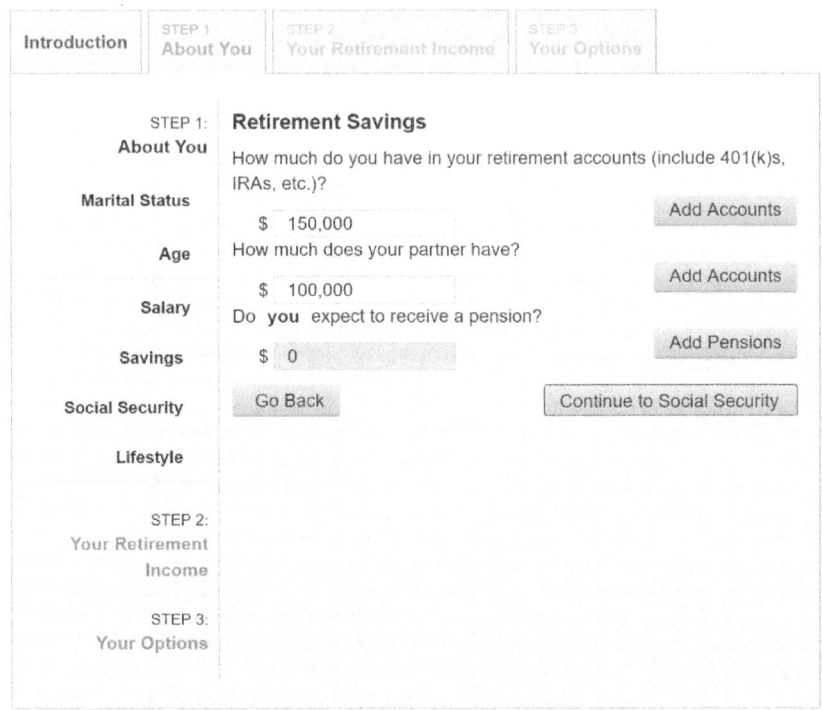

Source: AARP Retirement Calculator

Further along, you will be asked how much you will be expecting from social security benefits along with lifestyle expense expectations (Figures 3.4 & 3.5). The modest option adjusts the calculations for less spending, meaning eating at home or walking instead of using transportation. The more extravagant option factors in a lifestyle where dining out and taking frequent vacations are typical.

Figure 3.4: AARP Retirement Calculator Questions – Step 1d

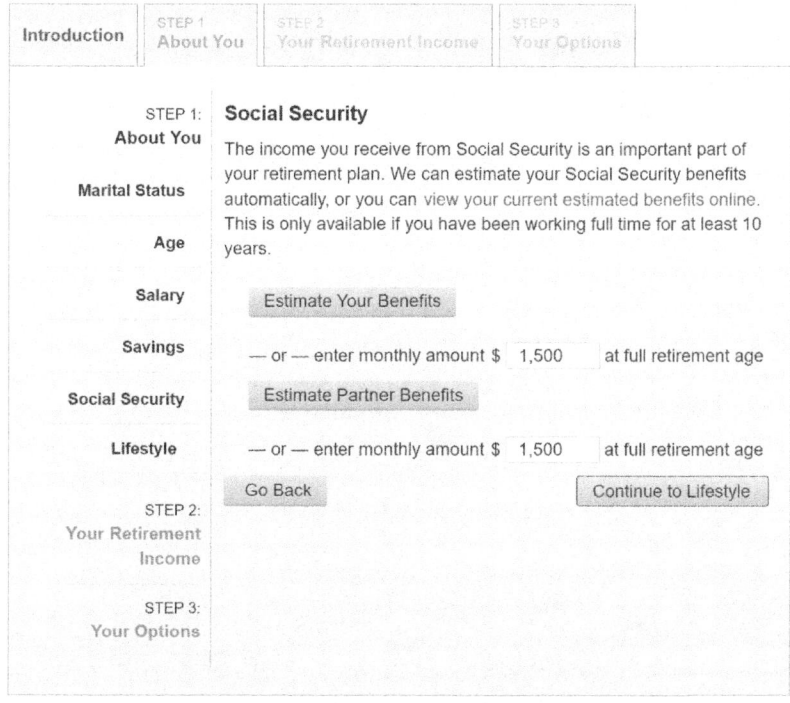

Source: AARP Retirement Calculator

Figure 3.5: AARP Retirement Calculator Questions – Step 1e

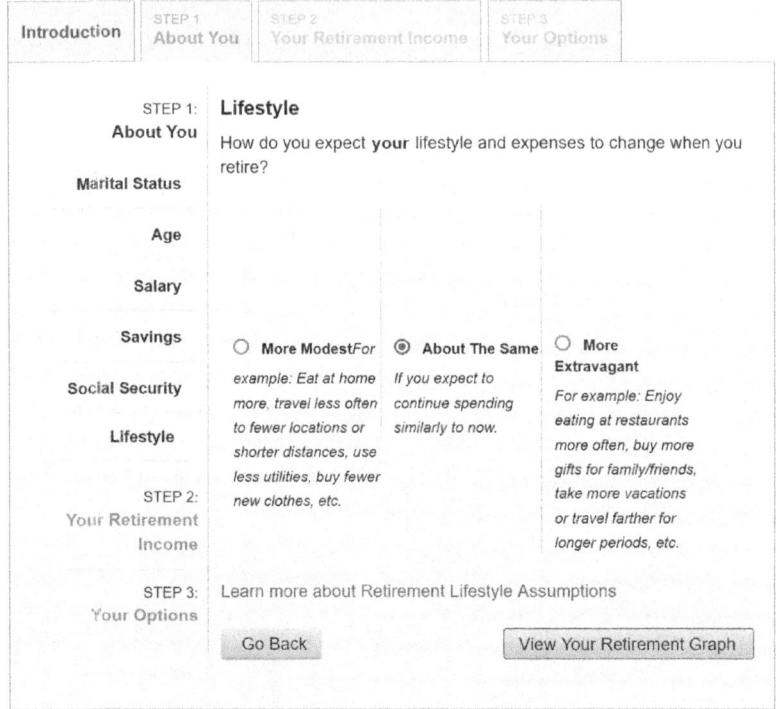

Source: AARP Retirement Calculator

Depending on your input and expectations, the calculator will tell you what lump sum you will need to retire to support your indicated lifestyle (Figure 4). The red-colored bars in the graph indicate at what age you are expected to run out of money. Money will become scarce at around 83 years of age in this example.

Figure 4: AARP Retirement Calculator Questions – Step 2

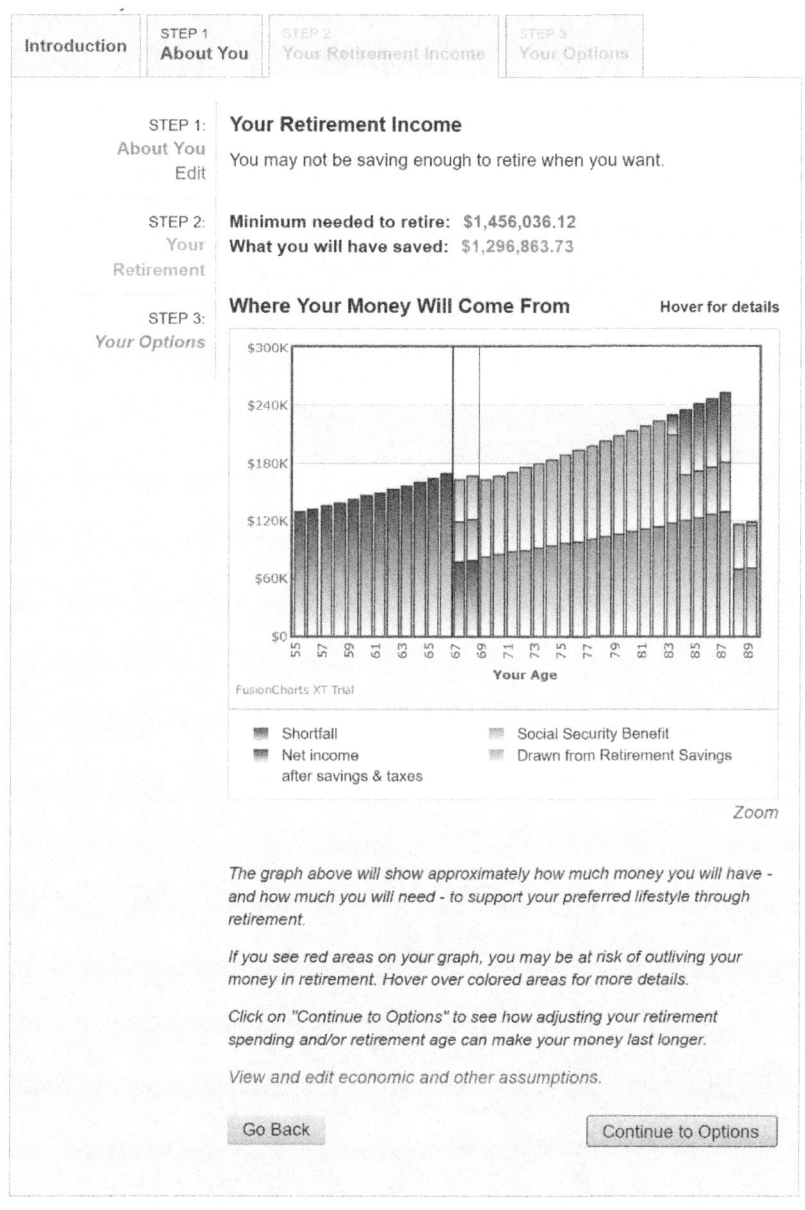

Source: AARP Retirement Calculator

The calculator automatically computes how much more or less you need to spend to ensure that you will remain within budget (Figure 5). From here, you can adjust your retirement spending and your targeted retirement age. Doing so will allow you to see how your money can last longer.

Figure 5: AARP Retirement Calculator Questions – Step 3

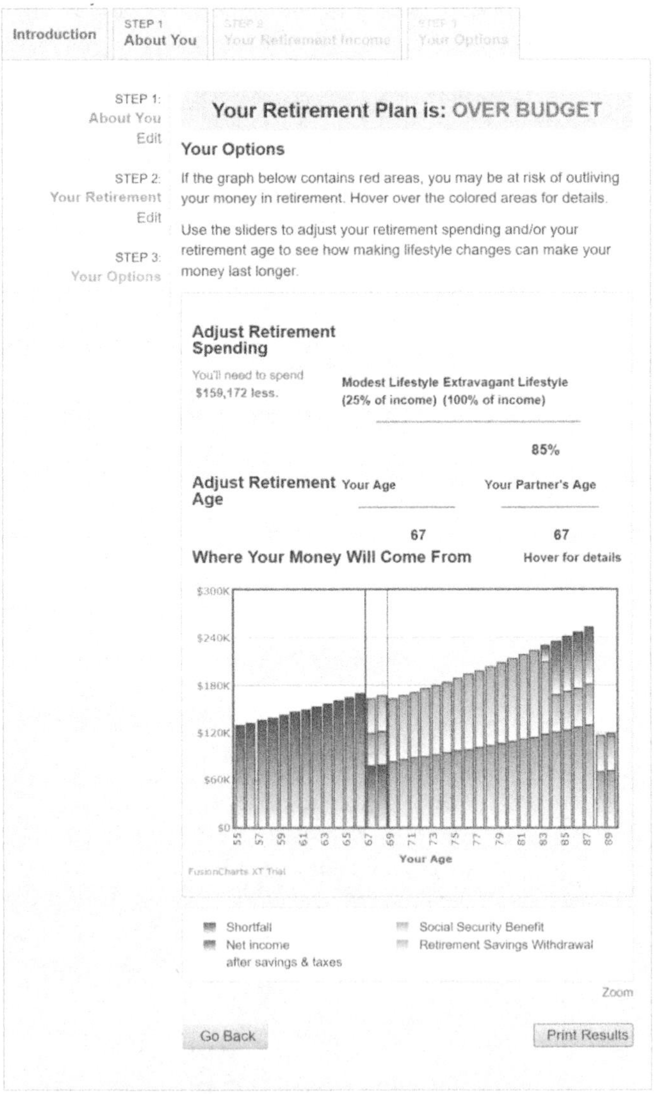

Source: AARP Retirement Calculator

Key Points:

1. The early retirement numbers can seem daunting (how much income is needed vs. how much income you can generate). However, do not worry – we will show you solutions to close the gap in the following chapters.
2. Online calculators help with fine-tuning your retirement plan, but the best one that I found was from AARP: https://www.aarp.org/work/retirement-planning/retirement_calculator.html

Next Chapter:

Did not save enough for retirement? Do not worry; you have options, and I will guide you through them.

CHAPTER 4
Your Options if You Have not Saved Enough

What you will learn in this chapter:

1. The available options if you have not saved enough for retirement.
2. How to supplement your retirement income and reduce mounting debt.

How much should you have saved for retirement by age 67?

Experts say you should have at least ten times your yearly salary saved up, while others say it should be double this.

The Bureau of Labor Statistics reports that the median weekly earnings in the U.S. for men aged 55 to 64 is $1,246 per week, while for women, it is $973.

Therefore, if we followed the advice of the experts, men should have at least $598,080 in their nest egg while women should have $467,040.

Do you have half a million dollars in your retirement savings account now? Will you by the time you retire at 67?

If you are like most retirees, the odds are that you are nowhere close to that number.

Understandably, you are concerned that you have not set aside enough and have no idea how to approach those numbers. Because of your age, you believe that you have less time to recover from any significant events or impacts on your financial situation. You also plan to work longer than the typical retirement age to ensure your paychecks continue to flow.

However, you do not have a backup plan if something happens, and you can no longer work at that job. Does this sound like you?

You are not alone with these fears because Transamerica Center for Retirement Studies revealed that 45% of baby boomers share the fear that they will outlive their savings and investments.

Their fears are typically due to not being aware of their options.

Do not worry because I have you covered. In the previous chapter, we discussed how much you needed for retirement. In this chapter we focus on what you can do if you do not have enough to even think about retiring. Those already retired who need a pathway towards a financially secured retirement can also benefit.

Option 1: Seek Professional Help

From EBRI research: "The drivers of retirement satisfaction and security appear to be guaranteed sources of income, low debt, a clear spend-down strategy, including advisory services."

This means that for you to live a financially stress-free retirement, you need to have: 1. Guaranteed income sources (no matter how small) 2. Low to no debt. 3. A clear spend-down strategy so when you withdraw money from your retirement savings, you do not touch the principal and allow your savings to grow over time.

This is not easy to achieve, but many have done it, and it is the goal of this book to teach you how.

Another good place to start is by discussing your situation with a financial advisor.

You probably think financial advisors are expensive. Unfortunately, most are, however, you can take advantage of several free resources.

The primary responsibility is to help people manage their income and reach their financial goals, whether they are already retired or looking to retire.

Choosing a financial advisor will take some time on your part to vet out. Fortunately for you, I have streamlined this process. Follow the steps below when choosing a financial advisor.

Understand the different types of financial advisors

a. Advisors specializing in retirement monthly income

Certain financial advisors are well-versed in helping clients generate high monthly income with low risk in retirement on small nest eggs.

They are agnostic to a particular fund or asset class and can show you the best-performing – low risk - monthly income strategies for retirement.

With several advisors in my network, you can get started for free.

You can go to my blog, "retirementmonthlyincome.com," and enter your contact information to get started.

b. Robo-advisors

Figure 6: Robo-advisor

It used to be that hiring a financial advisor meant that there was a person that you would be talking to. These days, Robo-advisors are prevalent, and they cater to those looking for quick and accessible 24/7 online financial planning. As the name implies, these Robo-advisors are not human but are instead software powered by artificial intelligence. They work by entering your personal information, and a retirement plan will be output based on your needs. Think of these as the next step after utilizing the retirement calculator. Again, the fees are meager at around 0.25% of your balance. Amazingly, some do not even have account minimums, so this is easily the most affordable on this list.

Granted, they have come a long way over the past decades, but they are limited in functionality. They are only as good as what you enter, so look elsewhere if you are not experienced in or intimidated by looking over numbers, especially budgeting, income expectations, or portfolio management. A personal connection cannot be made with Robo-advisors, so if there are any personal events or situations that you factored into your retirement planning, they would not be able to provide any guidance. Sofi and Betterment provide Robo-advisor services considered industry-leading, so make sure to start your research there.

c. Traditional Financial Advisors

Certified financial planners, registered investment advisors, financial consultants, stockbrokers, and wealth managers are all examples of traditional financial advisors. It is not uncommon to see financial advisors hold multiple titles as much of the work overlaps. For example, a certified financial planner may also be active as a retired investment advisor.

Expect to meet face-to-face with someone, usually at their office during regular business hours. You may prefer this route if you value personal feedback and recommendations from experience from a human personal advisor. However, they are limited in their service because they can only advise based on their experience and recommendations. Not all personal advisors are created equal, so you will need to do some due diligence and research in your area concerning whom you want to work with. Some financial advisors create a financial plan for you, and all you must do is execute it. Others will handhold you through the process, while some will offer their services for free, meaning they consider their time volunteer work. The choice is yours, but you will need to look for the one that applies to your needs. Look into NAPFA or Financial Planning Association to get you started.

When you find the right one, it should not surprise you that they will command high prices. Their requirements and fees will vary, so you must factor this in a while doing your research. Some will require a high minimum balance just to get started. For example, they may require that you have at least $250,000 in assets in your account before they commit to working with you. However, aside from the high cost, you get what you pay for: specialized service, advice based on personal experience, and a person who can empathize with you.

d. Online Financial Advisors

Right in the middle between Robo-advisors and traditional financial advisors are online financial advisors. Consider this option as the "best of both worlds." You get the automated investing planning that Robo-advisors provide while having customer support from an actual human financial advisor. However, the personal connection you make with traditional financial advisors may not be present with this hybrid option because there are usually teams of financial advisors behind the scenes. Some services offer personal advisors dedicated to your account, but you will have to do some research to find these.

Online financial advisors are best for those who understand their financial situation decently – enough so that they are at ease when entering data for the Robo-advisor-generated questions. Support is there when you ask for it, but it can be a bit of a boilerplate response. The cost falls in between a traditional financial advisor and Robo-advisor. The requirements and fees will vary but expect to see account minimum requirements range from $500 to upwards of $25,000. Wealthfront and Vanguard are well known for online financial advisors, so start your research here.

Option 2: Reduce Your Debt as Much as Possible

Experts agree that the number one factor for a stress-free retirement is to become debt-free. Studies have shown that retirees with low income and no debt are happier than retirees with high income and some debt.

Consider the following to gain control of your debt:

Create a budget

Experts agree that you should be dividing your after-tax income into three buckets. First, use the allocation strategy below to get a clear picture of your money needs. Then, based on your needs, adjust accordingly.

- 50% should go to *needs* such as paying for the mortgage, utilities, food, or healthcare
- 30% should go to *wants* such as dining out, going to the movies, or traveling
- 20% should go to *savings* such as 401(k) or emergency funds

As you get closer to retirement, you will need to prioritize your needs and savings over your wants.

Reduce Your Expenses

You may have debt from various sources: credit cards, medical, or utility bills. Because of your responsibility to pay back the loans you borrowed, you will need to find a way to do so without being delinquent on any of your monthly payments. It is not ideal, but you may have to reduce some of the creature comforts and luxuries you are accustomed to.

Do you go out to eat with your friends and family every week? Just remember that all those Sunday brunches add up over time. What about going out to the movie theater, skating, the local bar, or shopping? Understand that these are necessary for you to live. These are indeed categorized as wants. Itemize your expenses related to wants, then determine how much you spend per month on average.

What is that number? $200? $500? $1000? Think about how you can use that money to pay off your debt sooner rather than later. Because loans come with heavy interest rates, especially from credit cards with some approaching 35% APR, it is best to pay them off as soon as possible. To put it simply, the longer it takes for you to pay off your loans, the more you will be paying in the long run. When you are in retirement mode, the last thing you want in your mind is to think about your debt responsibilities.

Debt Settlement and Consolidation

How many creditors are mailing you monthly bills? Are you still paying off your auto loan, have medical bills, and have multiple credit cards? Managing all those expenses can be challenging and complicated because of the varying loan rates that each lender may charge. This makes it hard to track your finances if you are constantly working to pay off one bill but are bombarded by others. Talk to your financial advisor about debt settlement and debt consolidation. You can expect savings in the hundreds if not thousands per year. Here are the main differences between the two.

Debt Consolidation

Debt Consolidation is a process where you can combine all or some of your debts into a single consolidated loan. Instead of worrying about multiple bills, you can focus on paying off one. The lender will provide you with a loan upon application approval which you can then use to pay off all your existing debt. Of course, you will be taking on new debt from this lender. However, the benefit here is that you only must deal with one bill per month, and you stand to save a substantial amount of money by taking advantage of their lower interest rate.

If you have assets (i.e., car, house, insurance policy) that can be used as collateral, you can have loans with lower interest rates, but make sure you shop around and see which one works best for you. There are online-based services available but check with your local bank or credit union as a starting place since they can provide personalized services and in-person customer support.

Debt Settlement

Another strategy to manage your debt is to settle them. Debt settlement refers to asking your creditors to settle on a lower amount than what you owe. You are effectively asking them if you can pay less than what you owe. This approach requires an agreement from you and the lender on the terms outlined. If there is an agreement, you can choose to pay the settlement with a one-time lump sum or a series of installments.

Understand, however, that creditors are in no way, shape, or form obligated to settle with you, so prepare yourself for a rejection. Another note to consider is that you will need to have cash on hand so that you can pay off the installments; otherwise, penalties and interests will accrue. You will not want to miss any payments because they can take you to court if missing payments become frequent.

Financial Assistance Programs

Programs such as AARP's Daily Money Management (DMM) or NCOA's Economic Checkup provide options for retirees where financial assistance is available. Although they are like financial advisors, what is beneficial here is that they will help with paying bills, negotiating with creditors, help you with avoiding scams, and provide support for general financial management activities. So again, financial assistance is available, but you will have to qualify for these benefits.

Option 3: Reduce Housing Related Expenses and Consider Moving

Figure 7: Do You Need a Large Home?

Remember the example list we created to calculate retirement expenses? If you recall from our earlier example (refer to Table 2), total monthly expenses totaled $6,600. Housing-related expenses alone made up nearly 40% of these expected expenses at $2,500. Sure, you can reduce your expenses in other ways by cutting the number of times you go out to eat, staying home instead of traveling, or cutting cable TV out of your life. However, all these savings pale compared to the savings that can be had if you relocated to somewhere more affordable.

Downsize Your Home

What is your monthly mortgage payment? The U.S. Census Bureau's American Housing Survey reports that Americans pay a median monthly mortgage payment of $1,609. How far above or below are you relative to this? What would your retirement look like if you continued to keep paying your mortgage into your retirement? Do you need a six-bedroom house, three-car garage, and an acre of property? Or can you settle into a cozy single-story home or apartment complex?

Your kids have moved out, and it is only you, your spouse, and your dog. Chances are your need for a large home is not a need anymore, but rather a want. Consider downsizing the mortgage payments by switching to a smaller one. Smaller homes, apartments, and condominiums are excellent choices for downsizing. Moreover, they may come with added benefits such as not having to pay for lawn care, reducing your monthly payments, and not having to worry about doing any repairs or general maintenance. These were all hidden costs of owning a house that you no longer must worry about.

Do the math and compare your monthly housing-related expenses with that of a downsized home.

Better yet, do some simple math and consider how much you pay in taxes every year. The average American will pay around $2,500 in property taxes each year. Depending on where you live, property taxes will range anywhere from $587 a year to over $8,000 a year. Realize that you do not need your big house and save substantially on expenses every month if you downsize your home. Remember, your goal is to have a financially stable retirement, which could mean sacrificing your wants and replacing them with your needs.

Option 4: Move to a Different State or Country

If you find yourself in a situation where you do not see a way into a financially secure retirement, it may be time to consider moving to a different city or country. Doing so can save you thousands a year or even monthly. Let us consider what to consider when moving to a different state or country.

States

One of the key points to look at when moving to a city is the "tax burden" you will encounter just by living there. This "tax burden" number indicates how much you pay towards state and local taxes.

Table 4 shows the top ten states that have the highest tax burden. The higher the number, the more you will be paying in taxes. So, keep this in mind when looking for the next state to relocate to. In contrast, Table 5 shows the top ten states with the lowest tax burden.

Table 4: Tax Burden by State (Top 10 Worst)

Overall Rank (1=Highest)	State	Total Tax Burden (%)	Property Tax Burden (%)	Individual Income Tax Burden (%)	Total Sales & Excise Tax Burden (%)
1	New York	12.79%	4.40%	4.96%	3.43%
2	Hawaii	12.19%	2.45%	3.09%	6.65%
3	Vermont	10.75%	5.04%	2.41%	3.30%
4	Maine	10.50%	4.60%	2.45%	3.45%
5	Connecticut	10.44%	4.06%	3.56%	2.82%
6	Minnesota	9.99%	2.86%	3.68%	3.45%
7	New Jersey	9.98%	4.94%	2.47%	2.57%
8	Rhode Island	9.69%	4.44%	2.29%	2.96%
9	Illinois	9.52%	4.00%	2.11%	3.41%
10	California	9.48%	2.64%	3.78%	3.06%

Source: https://taxfoundation.org

Table 5: Tax Burden by State (Top 10 Best)

Overall Rank (1=Highest)	State	Total Tax Burden (%)	Property Tax Burden (%)	Individual Income Tax Burden (%)	Total Sales & Excise Tax Burden (%)
40	Montana	7.45%	3.59%	2.58%	1.28%
40	Alabama	7.45%	1.41%	1.96%	4.08%
43	South Dakota	7.37%	3.02%	0.00%	4.35%
44	Oklahoma	7.13%	1.67%	1.92%	3.54%
45	Florida	6.97%	2.74%	0.00%	4.23%
46	New Hampshire	6.84%	5.47%	0.13%	1.24%
47	Delaware	6.21%	1.77%	3.25%	1.19%
48	Wyoming	6.14%	3.33%	0.00%	2.81%
49	Tennessee	5.74%	1.70%	0.08%	3.96%
50	Alaska	5.10%	3.68%	0.00%	1.42%

Source: https://taxfoundation.org

Countries

If you feel adventurous, perhaps you should consider moving abroad to an affordable country. I have compiled a list of the top 10 places where you can live comfortably while keeping your expenses low at the same time. Consider what is available in these cities as well. How close are they to the beach? Do they have entertainment or activities that you are interested in? Can you carry over your hobbies when you settle in these countries? Of course, you will have to research these countries and their respective cities, but Table 6 should give you a good idea of living expense expectations.

Table 6: Top 10 List of Affordable Countries

Country	City	Average monthly local salary	Average monthly rent (1 bed; Center City)	Average monthly rent (Shared apt; Center City)	Cost of the meal (Inexpensive restaurant)	Cost of living (Compared to NYC)
Ecuador	Quito	$472	$392	$227	$3	70% cheaper
South Korea	Seoul	$2,390	$585	$504	$6	66% cheaper
China	Beijing	$1,035	$496	$359	$3	57% cheaper
Portugal	Lisbon	$1,011	$705	$400	$9	57% cheaper
Georgia	Tbilisi	$297	$263	$181	$5	80% cheaper
Spain	Madrid	$1,582	$776	$412	$13	50% cheaper
Cambodia	Phnom Penh	$214	$384	$317	$3	66% cheaper
Costa Rica	San José	$787	$501	$280	$7	65% cheaper
Morocco	Rabat	$458	$341	$195	$3	74% cheaper
Mexico	Mexico City	$475	$337	$222	$5	71% cheaper

Source: https://internationalliving.com/the-best-places-to-retire/

Option 5: Work Part-Time to Supplement Income in Retirement

Another great way to reduce the amount needed for retirement is to work part-time in your field of expertise or one you enjoy and want to learn more about.

Working part-time also gives your life a bit of structure without the stress.

Below are some of the best resources and websites focused on finding part-time jobs for retirees.

AARP Resources

The Work channel provides information and education to help people aged 50-plus find a job, tweak résumés, polish interviewing skills, negotiate a salary and benefits, explore a second career path, explore flexible work arrangements, consider self-employment, and more. It also features the SimplyHired job search tool, which lets you easily search by job title or company, as well as location.

AARP Foundation's Back to Work 50+ program helps older workers find better jobs by assisting with job training, career counseling, and networking. In addition, you can learn more about intelligent job-seeking strategies and gain the support of national and local job-assistance partners.

AARP's LifeReimagined offers a work program that includes tips on getting reinvigorated about your job, setting goals, and becoming your boss. In addition, you can take an online course that will help with your job search.

Additional Resources

- Workforce50.com: For job seekers 50 and over; formerly called Senior Job Bank.
- Retired Brains: For older boomers, seniors, and retirees.

- Seniors4Hire: For job seekers 50 and over.
- YourEncore: For older scientists, engineers, and product developers.
- RetireeWorkforce.com: For retirees and mature workers.
- USA Jobs: It lets you browse federal government job openings.
- The Riley Guide: Career advice plus links to thousands of websites that offer job postings and resources.
- Job-Hunt.org: Links to a wide range of employment websites and career resources.
- Weddle's: Internet resources on job hunting and career management; includes an online bookstore and bi-weekly newsletter.
- Quintessential Careers: Comprehensive site for job search and career advice. Use the search page to find articles geared to 50+ workers, including changing careers, résumés, age bias, and more.
- Wall Street Journal - Careers: The *Wall Street Journal's* executive career site. Find job postings, salary information, advice on managing your career, and an online forum.
- Career One-Stop Centers: Centers provide employment assistance to job seekers in over 2,000 communities across the U.S., offering to help with finding a job, planning your next career steps or change, locating training, and coping with job loss. To find one near you, call toll-free 877-US2-JOBS (877-872-5627).
- U.S. Small Business Administration (SBA): Provides information, one-on-one counseling, and training at no charge to individuals who seek to start a business. SBA centers are located throughout the country and have libraries, special services for women entrepreneurs, and access to market research databases.
- Social Security Administration (SSA): Find details on the earnings limit and other benefits issues.

- Execu-Net: Find job opportunities and networking for executive jobs in the $100K employment market. It requires paid membership (30-, 90-, 180- and 360-day options).
- 40Plus: A volunteer organization devoted to helping its members find jobs. It offers a training course, job search counseling, résumé development, weekly peer support meetings, and other resources, all supported by member fees.
- Five O'Clock Club: This is a career coaching and outplacement network for professionals, managers, and executives. It offers a five-volume set of job search books and presentations by professional career counselors. Members can attend weekly meetings or join by teleconference and network with other members. Membership fees are based on the number of sessions attended. Also, free articles are available on the website.

Key Points:

1. You can take many steps if you have not saved enough for retirement. The key is to get your debt to near 0. Leverage free debt forgiveness and consolidation services, downsizing your home, move to a cheaper state or country, working part-time in retirement
2. Next, use your small savings to generate the highest possible monthly income stream. You will need to do this safely, without touching the principal, so that the income will last you through all the years of retirement. How to do this is explained in the following chapters.

Next Chapter:

Given a particular nest egg (whether it is $100,000 or $2,000,000) – what are the best investment strategies to generate high monthly income so you can live off your savings without running out of money?

CHAPTER 5
The Dilemma Facing Retirees Today (Low Savings, Low Returns)

Ten years ago, investment advisors recommended a 60-40 investment portfolio (60% stocks to 40% bonds) for retirement. The thought was that with 60% of your money in stocks, you would have enough growth potential to meet your goals.

Moreover, with 40% in bonds, you will have a stable source of income to fall back on if your stocks do not perform.

Today, well-respected firms like Bank of America, Morgan Stanley, and JPMorgan have all proclaimed the death of the 60/40 rule.

David Kelly, Chief Global Strategist for J.P. Morgan Asset Management, says a "plain vanilla" portfolio of 60% global equities and 40% U.S. bonds is likely to net an annual return of just over 4% in the next 10 to 15 years. This is because bond yields (interest paid) today are tiny compared to 15 years ago.

For example, the return on a 10-year Treasury note reached a high of 15.84% back in 1981. By the end of the decade, it had fallen to 9.5%. It is currently hovering around *1.5%* — not that better than simple savings accounts.

To complicate things further,

- The stock market is at record levels with a probability of a significant correction high.
- In 2000 and 2008, retirees lost 40% of their savings on "safe" investments and took over 7+ years to make money back.
- Bonds pay next to nothing and, in some cases, provide negative yields.
- Cash has no return and is less than inflation.

Investors, therefore, face a dilemma on how to generate monthly income for their retirement needs.

What do investment managers suggest?

- Many investment managers suggest moving to risky alternative assets to generate higher returns, where fees can be high and strategies complex.
- I do not recommend this approach.

What are alternative assets comprised of?

Here are some common alternative investment types:

- Private equity – investing in private companies
- Venture capital – investing in private companies
- Private debt
- Hedge funds
- Real estate
- Commodities (for example, investing in wheat, gold, oil)

Investing in alternative assets often requires buyers to lock up their money for five, maybe ten years. During that time, investors may not see any money distributed.

What are the problems with alternate investments?

- Alternative investments and hedge funds involve **a high degree of risk** and can be challenging to buy and sell.
- They can be highly speculative and volatile, and an investor could lose all or a substantial investment.

So – what should a retiree do?

Fortunately, there is no need to take on risky and expensive alternate investments like private equity and commodities to generate high income in retirement. The subsequent chapters will show you exactly where to invest for a high monthly income with lower risk.

CHAPTER 6
Structure of the Next Chapters (High Income Strategies)

This chapter explains how the subsequent strategy chapters are laid out, making it easier to follow along. In addition, the concepts are simple to understand, and you do not need to have advanced financial knowledge to do so.

Please read the following chapters in sequence. In addition, I suggest reading the following chapters a few times to grasp the core concepts fully.

Chapter 7 is a glossary of key financial terms essential to understanding high monthly income strategies. You need to understand if a particular investment is good or bad, risky, or not.

Chapter 8 introduces the retirement bucket strategy, a great way to reduce risk further.

Chapter 9 analyzes the current high-income options available today and explains why most of them are too risky.

Chapter 10 is the book's core and shows you the four best investments for high monthly income with low risk in retirement. It includes my # 1 pick.

Chapters 11 and 12 spell out the high monthly income – low-risk strategy in clear steps so you can follow it easily. One is a passive, easy, set-it-and-forget-it strategy, and the other is an active strategy for higher returns.

Chapter 13 summarizes all the critical information, provides an action plan, and discusses the next steps.

CHAPTER 7
Basic Financial Terms to Understand

Below is a glossary of key financial terms. It will help you understand why specific income strategies are better than others. I suggest spending some time understanding these concepts.

If you have questions, email me at info@retirementmonthlyincom.com. I respond to every inquiry.

a. Risk

- It is critical to understand risk - when it comes to generating income in retirement.
- Typically, higher returns take on higher risk, but not always - as I will show you.
- Buying a basket of stocks (a mutual fund) is less risky than buying an individual stock.
- Buying indexes (S&P 500, Nasdaq, DOW) is less risky than buying a specific stock market sector (e.g., real estate, consumer goods, energy, technology, healthcare).
- You may get some great stock tips and read articles like "best dividend stocks paying over 9%" or "best sectors to invest in for high income," etc. but be warned that most of these investments are too risky.
- If you want to invest in the stock market, indexes like S&P 500, DOW, and Nasdaq are safer than most.

- Stock indexes are safer than stock sectors which are safer than individual stocks.

b. Understand the term "Beta."

- "Beta" is a quantitative measure of risk (or volatility) in an investment.
- The S&P 500 index has a beta value of 1.
- Higher the beta, the more the risk.
- Low-beta stocks (less than 1) pose less risk but typically have lower returns.
- I focus on low beta investments for retirement income as they have less risk. That means that if the index (e.g., SP500, Nasdaq.) drops 1%, investments with a low beta will drop less (e.g., 0.5%).
- However, if the index (SP500, Nasdaq) goes up 1%, the ETF with the low beta will go up less (e.g., 0.5%).

Key Points:

- In a highly overvalued stock market like today, look for low beta investments, as they are less volatile, and you will get downside protection which is crucial in retirement.
- In undervalued markets (typically after a significant correction), look for high beta investments to give you higher returns as the market turns.
- We show you the best investments for each market type in later chapters.

c. ETF (Exchange-Traded Fund)

An exchange-traded fund (ETF) is a collection of securities that trade on an exchange just like a stock does.

ETF share prices fluctuate all day as the ETF is bought and sold; this is different from mutual funds that only trade once a day after the market closes.

ETFs can contain all types of investments, including stocks, commodities, or bonds; some offer U.S.-only holdings, while others are international.

Key Points:

- An exchange-traded fund (ETF) is a basket of stocks - so it is inherently less risky than individual stocks.
- You can buy ETFs in all trading and retirement accounts. It is as easy as buying a stock. You just need the ticker symbol (e.g., VMBS, BLV) to trade it.

d. Yield, Dividend Yield, or Distributions (Income)

The dividend yield (or income) is how much interest a company pays per share of the stock owned. It is a crucial metric to watch for when investing for income.

Suppose Company A's stock is trading at $20 and pays annual dividends of $1 per share to its shareholders, while Company B's stock is trading at $40 and pays an annual dividend of $1 per share.

This means Company A's dividend yield is 5% ($1 / $20), while Company B's dividend yield is only 2.5% ($1 / $40).

So, in the above example, all things being equal, Company A pays out more than Company B.

Key Points:

- Dividends are a great way to receive income from your investments. Some pay monthly, others quarterly, or even annually.
- For retirement purposes, we will be focused on investments paying monthly.

e. How to Find the Dividend Payouts for any ETF

How do you find the amount of income paid by an ETF?

An easy way is to go to the ETF's website and see the distributions there. See Figure 8 for a sample on the Vanguard website.

Figure 8: How to find yield (income) of an investment

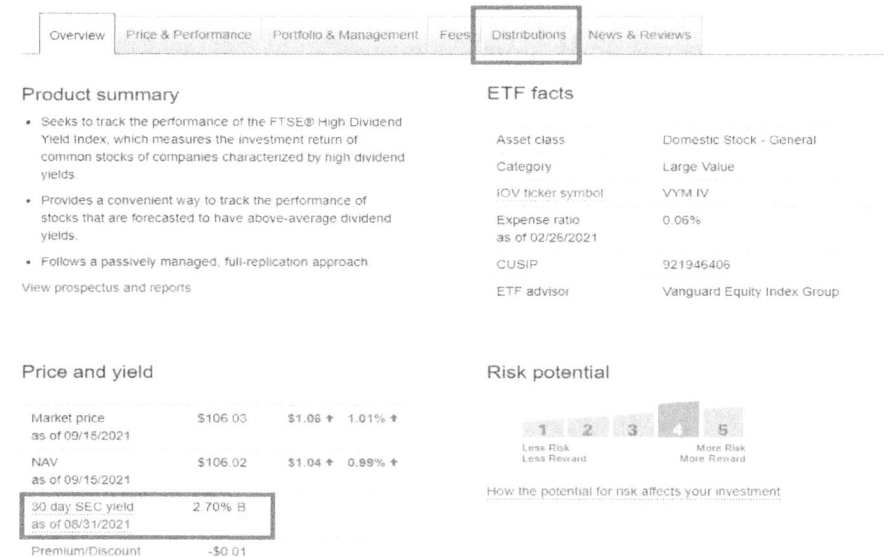

Source: Vanguard.com

You can see that the above ETF has dividends paid quarterly. So, on 06/24/2021, you will receive $0.7523 per share of VYM that you own. So, if you owned 1000 shares, you would receive $752 for the quarter.

Key Points:

1. It is crucial to understand and calculate how much each investment pays on either a monthly, quarterly, or annual basis.
2. In retirement, we want to focus on investments paying monthly.
3. In addition to how much the ETF (or any investment) is paying monthly, you will need to watch how the ETF performs when the stock market drops. Some drop 50% and are not suitable investments even though they pay high monthly dividends.

f. Fees

Another metric to watch for is fees. There are a lot of mutual funds, ETFs that pay monthly dividends (income) but charge high fees.

You can quickly review the management fees by going to Yahoo Finance, typing in the ETF or mutual fund's name, and viewing the fees. See Figure 9 to view the expense ratio (fees) of the LIT ETF.

Figure 9: How to find fees of an investment

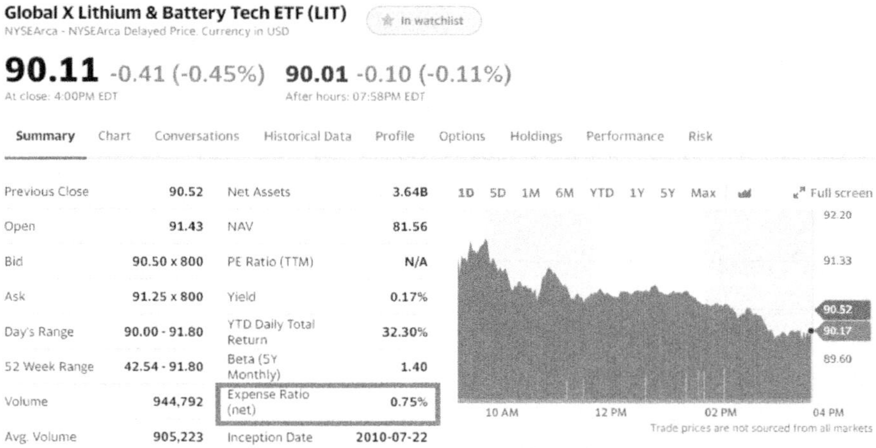

Source: Yahoo Finance (2022)

Key point:

- You want to look for ETFs that pay high monthly income, have downside protection (if the stock market drops) + low fees.

g. Overvalued, Undervalued market

It is essential to understand where you are in the stock market cycle. When the stock market is overvalued at all-time highs, you need to invest in non-risky assets.

Alternatively, when the market is undervalued (typically after a significant correction), you can invest in more risky assets that generate higher returns as markets always go up over time.

We are currently in an overvalued market, so you need to pay attention to risk and invest in ETFs that protect you from large stock market drops.

As seen in Figure 10, the U.S. stock market is now as expensive as any time in its history - except for the dot-com bubble:

Figure 10: How to Tell if Stock Market is Overvalued or undervalued

Shiller PE Ratio

Source: https://www.multpl.com/shiller-pe

According to the Shiller CAPE Ratio (which measures PE or Price to Earnings Ratios), the U.S. stock market is now as expensive as any time in its history - except for the dot-com bubble:

Key point:

- We are currently in a highly overvalued market. It does not mean the market will not keep going up, but retirees should invest for high monthly income AND *downside protection* should there be a significant drop.

h. Options and Covered Calls for monthly income

Options are complex, but it is good to understand them at a high level - as it is a great way to generate high monthly income with low risk. For example, experts agree that selling covered calls on quality stocks and ETFs is safe to generate monthly income, as the money you get from selling a covered call is guaranteed.

Generating monthly income via options used to be reserved for the few financial gurus that understood it but are now open to anyone.

In addition, there are new covered call ETF's which you can buy just like a stock and collect the monthly income for a low fee without doing any of the heavy lifting.

Investing in these covered call ETF's is core to the strategies we will show you in the following chapters.

What is an Option?

Before getting into covered calls, it is essential to know what an option is. An option is simply a contract between a buyer and a seller. The option seller (also known as the option writer) sells an option to the buyer. The option gives the seller the obligation to do something should the buyer request it.

What is a Call Option?

A call option is a contract where the buyer has a right (but not an obligation) to purchase an item (in this case, shares) at a set price. However, the seller is obliged to sell the item if the buyer requests it (called exercising).

What Is a Covered Call?

It is best explained as an example:

Let us take John, Sue, and a pound of corn worth $10/pound today.

John has a pound of corn and wants to sell someone an option to purchase his pound of corn in one month for $10. John thinks the price of corn will be about the same or lower (next month) than it is today.

On the other hand, Sue thinks the price of a pound of corn will likely go up next month. So, Sue agrees with Jimmy to buy his pound of corn in 1 month. In return, Sue pays John a fee for this contract (this is the covered call). Sue and John negotiate a fee of $1 for this option. The $1 is the income (option premium) that John gets to keep, no matter how much the beans go up or down in value.

John collects the $1 and agrees to sell Sue his pound of corn next month for $10.

Next month, if a pound of corn cost more than $10, Sue will buy the corn from John for $10. Otherwise, if the corn costs less than $10, her option contract is worthless. Whatever happens, John gets to keep his income (option premium) from Sue.

Key Points:

- You do not need to understand how options work in detail; however, be aware that covered calls are an

- excellent strategy for generating a high monthly income with low risk.
- In addition, with new investments on the market, investing in covered calls is as easy as buying a stock.

i. ELNs (Equity Linked Notes) for monthly income

Equity-linked notes are also complex. You do not need to understand the inner workings, but having a high-level understanding is essential as it is also a great way to generate safe and high monthly income.

Equity-linked notes allow investors to protect their capital while also getting the potential for an above-average return compared to regular bonds.

In theory, the upside potential for returns in an equity-linked note is unlimited, whereas the downside risk is capped.

Benefits of Equity-Linked Notes

1. Opportunity to earn higher interest income

Investors want to invest in equities because they have historically outperformed fixed-income investments. In addition, equity-linked notes allow higher returns than fixed-income investments, such as guaranteed investment certificates (GICs).

2. Lower risk due to principal protection

Most equity-linked notes allow investors to protect their capital, and it is common for them to offer complete principal protection. As a result, it makes ELNs appealing to risk-averse investors who want to explore equity markets with a safety net.

Key Point:

- ELNs are another excellent way for risk-averse investors to generate high monthly income.

j. CEF - Closed-end funds

Examples: GDV, EXG

Like many mutual funds, a closed-end fund has a professional manager overseeing the portfolio and actively buying, selling, and holding assets.

Like any stock or ETF, its shares fluctuate in price throughout the trading day. However, the closed-end fund's parent company will issue no additional shares, and the fund itself will not buy back shares.

Closed-end funds and open-end mutual funds have many similarities. For example, both make income distributions and capital gains to their shareholders. Moreover, the companies that offer them must be registered with the Securities and Exchange Commission (SEC).

Pros: *high yield/monthly interest Cons: high volatility + high risk*

Key Points:

- Closed-End Funds can generate high yields for monthly income, but they are volatile and high risk, especially in bear markets where some have lost over half their value.
- Therefore, I am not a fan of CEF's for retirement income.

k. Business Development Corporations

Business Development Companies make debt and equity investments in other companies, typically small or mid-size businesses. These target companies may not have access to traditional means of raising capital, making them suitable partners for a BDC. BDCs invest in various companies, including turnarounds, developing, or distressed companies.

BDCs make money by investing to generate income and capital gains on their investments when they are sold. In this way, BDCs operate similar business models as private equity firms or venture capital firms.

However, the significant difference is that private equity and venture capital investment are typically restricted to accredited investors, while anyone can invest in publicly traded BDCs.

The appeal for BDCs is their high dividend yields. It is not uncommon to find BDCs with dividend yields above 5%. In some cases, certain BDCs provide 10%+ yields.

Key points:

- BDCs, just like CEFs - can generate high yields for monthly income, but they are volatile and high risk, especially in bear markets where some have lost over half their value.
- Therefore, we are not a fan of CEF's retirement income.

I. REIT (Real Estate Investment Trust)

REITs offer investors of all sizes an easy way to add the historically strong investment class of real estate to their investment portfolios.

What *are* REITs exactly? A REIT is a company that makes investments in income-producing real estate. Investors can buy shares of a REIT and, through that share ownership, effectively add the real estate owned by the REIT to their investment portfolios.

REITs can be classified in 3 ways:

1. By the types of investments they pursue (i.e., equity or debt, such as a mortgage REIT).
2. By how their shares are traded (i.e., exchange-traded REITs or non-listed REITs).
3. By the real estate sectors on which they focus (i.e., healthcare REITs or industrial REITs).

REITs historically have delivered total competitive returns based on high, steady dividend income and long-term capital appreciation. There is a comparatively low correlation with other assets

Key Point:

- REITs can generate medium yields (monthly income), but they are somewhat risky and have lost 40% of their value in 2008 (mortgage crisis) and during the pandemic in March 2020. However, they have since recovered.

m. BONDS

Bonds are also sometimes called "fixed income" assets. They broadly refer to investments that pay investors fixed interest or dividend payments until they mature. At maturity, investors are repaid the principal amount they had invested.

Government and corporate bonds are the most common types of fixed-income products.

Investment advisors typically recommend a 60-40 stock to a bond investment portfolio. However, there is much press regarding this being a risky and non-performing strategy for the next ten years due to low bond yields and an overvalued stock market.

Here are the most common types of fixed income products:

- **Treasury bills** are short-term fixed-income securities that mature within one year.
- **Treasury Inflation-Protected Securities** protect investors from inflation.
- **Municipal Bonds** are similar to a Treasury since it is government-issued, except it is issued and backed by a state, municipality, or county instead of the federal government.
- **Corporate Bonds** come in various types, and the price and interest rate offered largely depends on the company's financial stability and its creditworthiness.
- **Junk Bonds** are also called high-yield bonds—are corporate issues that pay a higher rate due to the higher risk of default. Default is when a company fails to pay back the principal and interest.
- A **certificate of deposit** is a fixed income vehicle offered by financial institutions with maturities of less than five years. The rate is higher than a typical saving account, and CDs carry FDIC or National Credit Union Administration (NCUA) protection.
- **Fixed-income mutual funds**—such as those offered by Vanguard—invest in various bonds and debt instruments. These funds allow the investor to have an income stream with the professional management of the portfolio. However, they will pay a fee for convenience.

Key Points:

- Bonds were recommended as a great way to generate monthly income in retirement.
- This is no longer the case, with bonds paying 1-3% (less than inflation) today.
- There are better options as well will show you in the following chapters.

CHAPTER 8
The Bucket Strategy and Why It is Important

Before discussing specific investments we like for high monthly retirement income, it is good to understand the bucket strategy and how it can be effectively applied to withdraw monthly income safely and reduce risk in retirement.

In a nutshell, to live off your savings, you will need to keep some money in stocks to keep parts of your portfolio growing even as you live off those investments. However, if there is a significant stock market correction in your retirement years, you may have to sell stocks or other assets while their values are down.

However, not holding stocks comes with its own set of risks. If your portfolio's growth cannot outpace inflation, you are more likely to outlive your money. If you are looking for a plan to let you invest for growth while keeping the money you will need in the near term safe from volatility; a bucket strategy is a good option.

The Bucket Strategy Advisors Recommend and Why It Does Not Work

Advisors recommend dividing your retirement assets into three categories based on when you will draw down on them.

1. The first bucket is for the money you intend to spend very soon (over the next year or two). This money should not be invested and keep it safe in cash.

2. The next bucket is for the portion of your portfolio that you expect to use in the medium term -- say, from two to 10 years in the future. You can invest this money but not in assets that are apt to fluctuate too much. This bucket should be made up of fixed-income investments like bonds.

3. The last bucket is for growth. Money that you do not expect to use for at least ten years can be invested in instruments like stocks that will provide you with higher long-term rates of return. Even if there is a market crash during your retirement, you will be able to hold onto those stocks for quite some time, which should give your portfolio time to recover. As bucket one runs low, you will replenish it from bucket two, which in turn should be topped off by shifting money from bucket three.

Problems with this approach

Let us say that you have $500,000 saved for retirement. Given the approach advisors recommend, here is the breakdown.

Here is an example of advisor recommendations:

To start: Divide your $500K portfolio into three buckets.

Bucket 1 - Money needed for the first 1-2 years (Cash)

Bucket 2 - half in fixed income

Bucket 3 – rest in stocks

Given the recommended approach (starting with $500,000), your total return will be only 4-5% even if the stock portion returns 8+%.

Table 7 below shows the strategy most advisors recommend and the problems with the recommended approach.

Table 7: Bucket Strategy most Advisors Recommend

Bucket Numbers	Years	Amount	Problem with this approach
1	1-2 years	$25,000 (cash)	Collects no interest
2	3-10 years	$200,000 (fixed income, bonds)	Returns 1-2%
3	10+ years	$275,000 (stocks)	Assume 8% return (unlikely with market overvalued)

Total Return is a low 4-5% or only ~$20,000/year in income.

The good news is that there is a better way, as you will see in the next section.

Recommended Approach

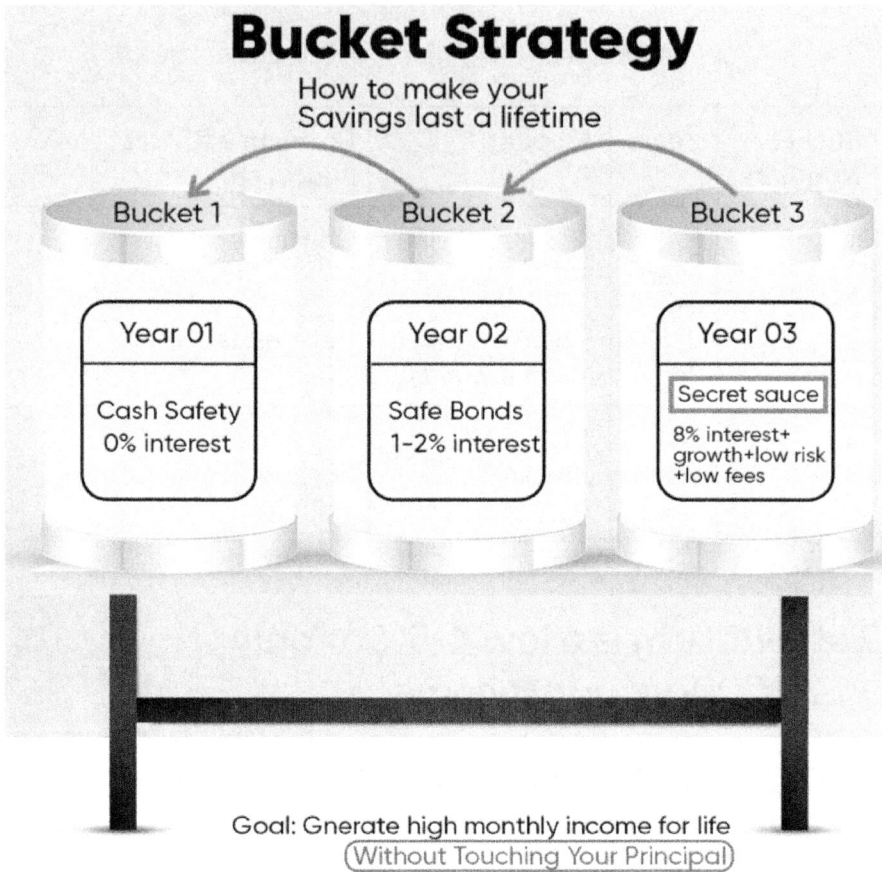

Here is what I recommend: with an example of $500,000: total return 7.5%+, no need to touch the bulk of principal.

Table 8 below shows my recommended approach on a $500,000 portfolio.

Table 8: Bucket Strategy I Recommend

Bucket Numbers	Years	Amount	Why this works
1	1st year	$25,000 (cash)	Safe for spending
2	2nd year	$25,000 (fixed income, safe, earns 1.3% e.g., VMBS)	Safe. Every year, move to bucket 1
3	3rd year onwards	$450,000 (8% yield + downside protection + some growth)	Invest in covered calls with downside protection (explained in the next chapters). Every year, take income money from this bucket (~36,000) and move it to bucket 2. *Done right; you can generate $36,000 per year + never have to touch your principal.*

Here is the bucket approach I recommend on a $500,000 portfolio:

1. **Bucket 1**: Living expenses of 5% ($25,000) in cash for Year 1.
2. **Bucket 2**: Living expenses of 5% ($25,000) in safe bonds (e.g., BIV) for Year 2.

3. **Bucket 3**: $450,000 invested in ETFs with high yield, downside protection, + growth.

With this approach, you can get $36,000 per year for living expenses without touching your principal.

Every year, move money from income earned in bucket 3 to bucket two and from bucket 2 to bucket 1.

Benefits:

- It is a safe strategy even if the market drops short term (longer-term market always goes up).
- Because you have safe investments in your first two buckets for at least 2 years, even if the market drops significantly in the 3rd bucket (your stock portfolio), you have time to weather the storm while collecting high income on the way.
- Done right, you do not have to touch your principal, only live off the interest
- *The key here is finding an investment (for bucket 3) that generates high income, low risk, growth, and downside protection. We will show you how in the following chapters.*

CHAPTER 9
Available High-Income Investments (With Pros/Cons of Each)

What you will learn:

1. There are many high-income investment options available today.
2. Unfortunately, most are high risk - where some investments have lost over 50% of their value in bear markets.
3. We show you which high monthly income investments are better than others and why.

You may have seen headlines like these: "The safest 8% dividend yield in the market," "Top three Extreme Dividend stocks that could supercharge your portfolio," or "#1 dividend stock for a LIFETIME of income."

There is an inherent risk in investing in a single stock or some high-yield investments. Many of these stocks and ETFs fare well in bull markets but lose 40-50% of their value in bear markets.

The goal in retirement is to find high monthly dividend investments that have downside protection, so you do not lose significant amounts of your principal in retirement – causing you to panic sell at the low.

Below are the options available to you as an investor, and we outline the pros and cons of each.

Option 1: High Dividend Stocks

> *Pros:* Several high dividend stocks exist
> *Cons:* High inherent risk, No downside protection

Many stocks pay high dividends, especially in real estate or business development corporations. However, individual stocks are inherently riskier than ETFs or Mutual Funds (baskets of stocks –less risk).

Take, for example, the pandemic in March 2020. Several high-income stocks lost over 50% of their value, and many investors panicked and sold low. If you own an ETF or mutual fund, you are less likely to panic sell during down markets as you have taken inherently less risk.

Take, for example, LTC Properties, Inc. (NYSE: LTC)

Dividend Yield: 6.68%

LTC Properties, Inc. (NYSE: LTC), a healthcare REIT, invests in seniors housing and healthcare properties through sale-leasebacks, mortgage financing, joint ventures, and structured finance solutions, including preferred equity and mezzanine lending.

Figure 11: Graph showing LTC Properties (a top dividend stock) down over 40% during the March 2020 pandemic

Source: https://www.google.com/finance/quote/LTC:NYSE?window=5Y

Figure 11 shows that LTC, like many other high-income stocks, lost over 40% of its value in March 2020 and has not fully recovered.

There are many stocks in a similar situation; some have recovered from the March 2020 pandemic lows while others have not.

I do not recommend high dividend income stocks for a novice retiree as they are too risky.

Option 2: Dividend income funds like Vanguard High Dividend ETF (VYM)

Pros: Safer than individual stocks
Cons: Low Yield (only 2.7%), No Downside Protection

Another option for a monthly income that is safer than buying individual stocks is a dividend or income ETF. For example, the Vanguard High Dividend Yield is a diversified income ETF. However, it pays only a 2.7% dividend and has no downside protection.

Figure 12: Graph showing a high-quality dividend ETF down over 40% during the March 2020 pandemic

Source:https://www.google.com/fnance/quote/VYM:NYSEARCA?window=5Y

Figure 12 shows VYM (Vanguard High Dividend ETF) losing over 30% during the March pandemic. Nevertheless, it pays a 2.8% dividend yield—medium risk for medium return.

Option 3: Utility ETFs (e.g., Vanguard Utilities Index Fund – VPU)

Pros: Average Yield
Cons: Moderate to High Risk, No Downside Protection

Utilities are typically deemed safe investments with good monthly income. Utilities refer to primary, regulated public services like water, natural gas, electricity, and sewage. The utility sector invests in long-term investors with stable income from dividends, lower volatility, and low correlation relative to the total stock market. Utilities also tend to perform okay during market downturns, as demand for utilities is relatively constant.

Figure 13: Graph showing a high-quality Utility sector ETF down over 30% during the March 2020 pandemic and paying only a 2.8% dividend

Source: https://www.google.com/finance/quote/VPU:NYSEARCA?window=5Y

Figure 13 shows Vanguard Utilities ETF performance during the March 2020 pandemic period, where it lost over 30% and has never fully recovered since. I am not a fan of utility stocks.

Option 4: Bonds (e.g., Vanguard Long Term Bond)

Pros: Moderate Income (2.8%)
Cons: Moderate Risk, yields less than inflation

As mentioned earlier, there are many types of bonds available for investing. They produce a moderate income and have moderate risk. However, today, bond yields are meager, and you will be hard-pressed to find bonds that pay anything over 3%. In addition, there is much press around the 60-40 portfolio being ineffective due to generationally low yields.

Bottom line: Good for safety, but monthly income is too low.

Option 5: MLPs, BDCs, and CEFs

Pros: High Income (5-11+%)
Cons: High Risk

Master Limited Partnerships, Business Development Corporations, and Closed-End Funds all provide high yields but have high risk, and some have lost over 50% of their value in down markets.

Here are some of the best MLPs, BDCs, and CEFs, and you can see their performance in a bear market.

Figure 14 shows Master Limited Partnerships (MLPs) – Ticker MLPX – a top-rated MLP lost 50% of its value in March 2020 and has not fully recovered.

Figure 14: Graph showing a high-quality MLP ETF down over 50% during the March 2020 pandemic and not fully recovering

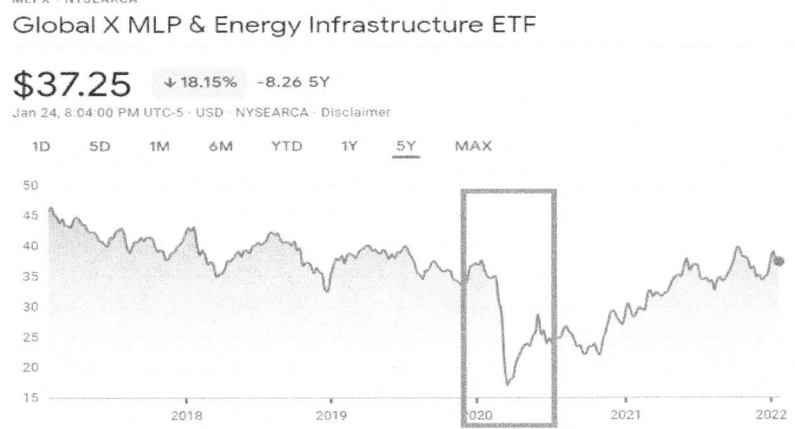

Source: https://www.google.com/finance/quote/MLPX:NYSEARCA?window=5Y

Business Development Corporation (BDCs) – Ticker GSBD – Goldman Sachs BDC lost over 40% of its value in March 2020 and has never fully recovered. See Figure 15 below for a BDC and Figure 16 for a top CEF that lost 40% of its value during the March pandemic.

Figure 15: Graph showing a high-quality MLP BDC down over 40% during the March 2020 pandemic and not fully recovering

Source: https://www.google.com/finance/quote/GSBD:NYSE?window=5Y

Figure 16: Graph showing a top Closed-End Funds losing over 40% of its value in March 2020 and not fully recovering

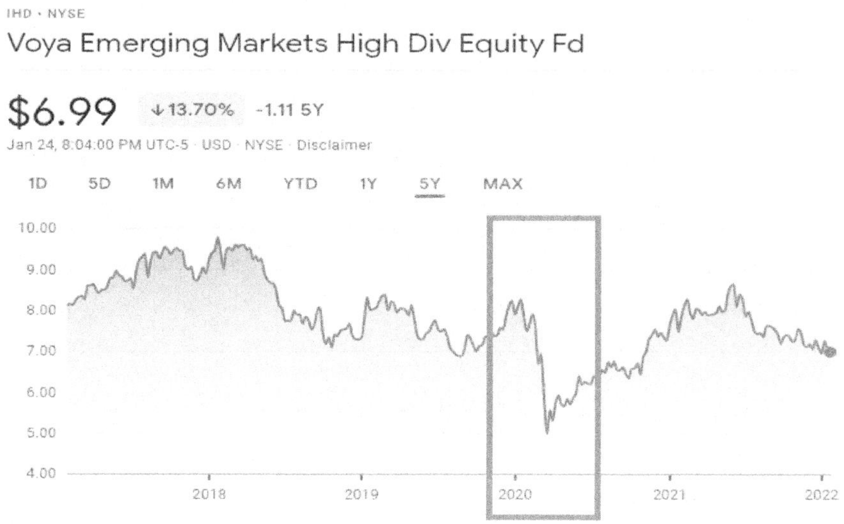

IHD · NYSE
Voya Emerging Markets High Div Equity Fd
$6.99
↓13.70%
-1.11 5Y
Jan 24, 8:04:00 PM UTC-5 · USD · NYSE · Disclaimer
1D
5D
1M
6M
YTD
1Y
5Y
MAX
10.00
9.00
8.00
7.00
6.00
5.00
4.00
2018
2019
2020
2021
2022

Source: https://www.google.com/finance/quote/IHD:NYSE?window=5Y

Option 6: Annuities

> ***Pros:*** *Guaranteed Income*
> ***Cons:*** *High risk, high fees, loss of principal*

Annuities promise lifetime guaranteed monthly or annual income for a retiree until their death. This sounds good on surface but beware high fees and early withdrawal penalties.

Pros:

Income for Life — The big draw to annuities is the fact that you get income for life no matter how old you are. Some people supplement with social security to receive a larger guaranteed income for life.

Fixed Rates —The payout from variable annuities depends on how the market performs, but with the fixed type, you know what your rate of return will be for a certain period. For older adults looking for a predictable income stream, that may be a better alternative than putting money into equities or even corporate bonds.

Cons:

High Fees — Fees over 2% are common and typically the fees you pay are complex and not transparent.

Surrender Fee and Complexity — Many annuities come with surrender fee, which you incur if you try to take a withdrawal within the first few years of your contract. Typically, the surrender period lasts between six to eight years, although they're sometimes even longer.

To summarize – Table 9 below shows the options available for retirees looking for high-income today:

Table 9: Monthly Income Investment Options for Retirees

Retirement Income Investments	Risk	Yield (Monthly income)	Any downside protection?
Individual dividend income stocks	Very High	Low-High (~1-10+ %)	no
Bonds	Medium	Low (1-3%)	no
Dividend Income ETFs	Medium	Medium (1-4%)	no
Annuities	Medium	2-6%	Yes
Utilities	Medium	Medium	no

BDCs (Business Development Corporation)	High	High ~7%	no
CEF (Closed-End Funds)	High	High ~7%	no
MLPs (Master Limited Partnerships)	High	High ~7+	no
Covered Call ETFs	Low-Medium	High ~7-11%	Yes, for some

As you can guess, we favor the <u>last row</u> - covered call ETFs and ELN ETFs for high monthly income with lower risk (i.e., with downside protection). I will show you why in the following chapters.

Recommended Investments for High Monthly Income

Investments for high monthly income	Risk	Monthly income	Recommended?
Individual income stock	High	Low 1-8%	No (too risky)
Bonds	Medium	1-3%	No (low income)
Dividend Income ETFs	Medium	Low-Medium	No (low income)
Utilities	Medium	Medium	No (medium income, medium risk)
BDCs (Business Development Corporation)	High	High 7%+	No (too risky)
CEF (Close-End Funds)	High	High 7%+	No (too risky)
MLPs (Master Limited Partnership)	High	High 7%+	No (too risky)
Annuities	Low	Low 3-6%	No (high fees, not transparent)
Covered Calls	Low to Medium	High 7-11%+	Yes, I show you the best ones

CHAPTER 10
Best Investments for Early Retirement (incl. #1 Pick)

To recap - below is the criteria to use when investing for monthly retirement income. The investment should provide:

- High monthly income
- Low risk
- Low fees
- Downside protection (given we are in an overvalued market today)

There are very few investments that meet these criteria.

Of all the available high-income investment options we went through in the last chapter, *high-quality* covered calls investments are your best bet. Covered calls used to be complex to understand and trade, but with new investments hitting the market – it is as easy as buying a stock.

Before recommending them, I constantly evaluate how each covered call investment performs during both bull and bear markets.

I will show you my top four covered call ETFs (Exchange Traded Funds) for high monthly income below. All four use covered calls or ELNs to generate income.

Two of the four have downside protection but lower yields (~8%).

The other two have no downside protection but higher income (~11%).

In an undervalued stock market, you will want to buy the ETFs with higher income (QYLD and RYLD yielding 11%), while in an overvalued stock market (like today), you will want to buy the ones with downside protection (JEPI and NUSI yielding ~8%).

Table 10 below shows the ranking for my top four covered call ETF's, and I indicate when to use which investment.

Table 10: (Ranking of Best Investments for High Monthly Income with Low Risk)

Ranking	ETF Ticker	Strategy	Downside Protection?	Yield (Income)	Management Fees	Risk (Beta)	When to use
1	JEPI	ELN's (tracks S&P 500 index)	Yes	~8%	0.36	Low (0.5)	Use for safe high monthly income + capital appreciation + downside protection
2	NUSI	Covered Calls (tracks Nasdaq 100 index)	Yes	~7.5%	0.68	Low (0.44)	Use for safe high monthly income + small capital appreciation + downside protection
3	QYLD	Covered Calls (tracks Nasdaq 100 index)	No	~11.8%	0.6	Medium (0.72)	Use in undervalued markets for high monthly income + capital appreciation
4	RYLD	Covered Calls (tracks Russell 2000 index)	No	~12%	0.6	Medium (0.64)	Use in undervalued markets for high monthly income + capital appreciation

Key Points:

- JEPI and NUSI are perfect for generating high monthly income investments with low risk in retirement.
- Use JEPI and NUSI for a safe set-it-and-forget-it strategy. In overvalued markets like today (2022) there is a strong probability of a large correction and JEPI gives you low volatility + downside protection, growth, high income, and reasonable fees.
- In **undervalued** markets, I recommend QYLD and RYLD due to the higher yield (income) and the higher appreciation expected once the market turns.

Figure 17 below shows that JEPI has the **least volatile** swings and is the best performer year to date (amongst the 4).

Figure 17: Graph showing JEPI having the least volatile swings when compared to other covered call ETF's

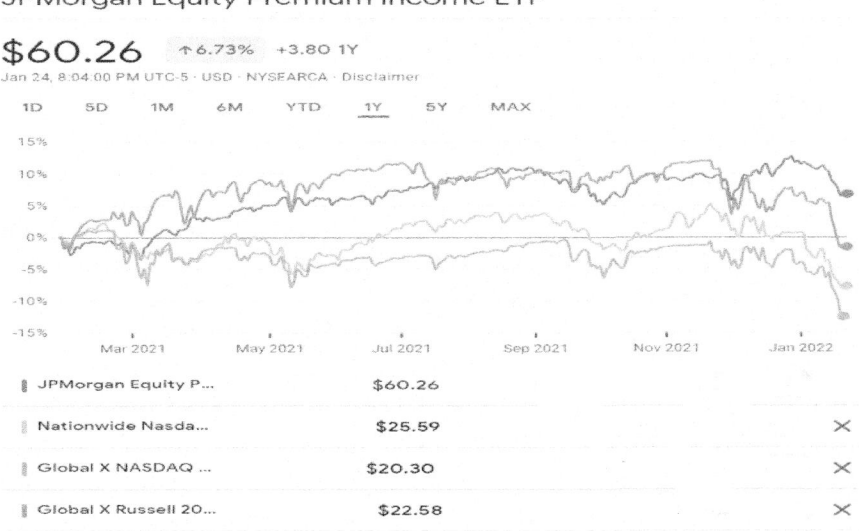

Source: https://www.google.com/finance/quote/JEPI:NYSEARCA?comparison=NYSEARCA%3ANUSI%2CNASDAQ%3AQYLD%2CBATS%3ARYLD&window=1Y

Figure 18 below shows how NUSI performed best (compared to QYLD and RYLD) if the bear market of March 2020 is included. JEPI is new, and there is insufficient data for JEPI in March 2020.

Figure 18: Graph showing NUSI dropping less than other covered call ETF's like QYLD and RYLD (which have no downside protection)

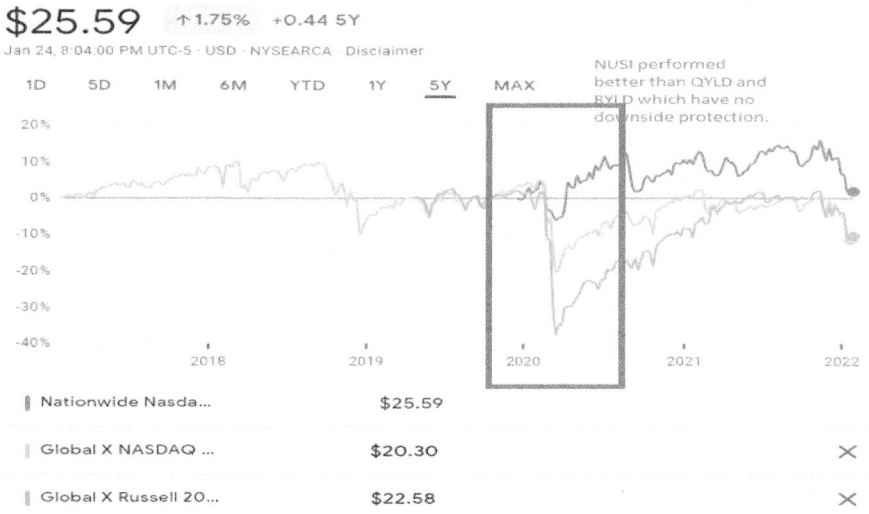

Source: https://www.google.com/finance/quote/NUSI:NYSEARCA?comparison=NASDAQ%3AQYLD%2CBATS%3ARYLD&window=5Y

Key Points:

- If we are in an overvalued market like today, you need downside protection as the risk of a correction is high. So NUSI and JEPI are safer bets as they have downside protection - which RYLD and QYLD do not.
- If we are in an undervalued market (for example - 2000 or 2008 – after a steep stock market drop), RYLD and QYLD will result in greater appreciation as the market

turns. However, RYLD and QYLD do not have downside protection and are more volatile.
- All 4 provide income ranging from 7.5%-11.5% per year.
- All four investments piggyback on the SP500 index, Russell 2000 index, or Nasdaq 100 index, which are inherently less risky than buying individual stocks.
- The major indexes *always* go up over time, so you get overall growth + high monthly income with these investments.

Essential information on the four recommended funds:

#1 Pick: JPMorgan Equity Premium Income ETF (JEPI)

Key Facts: **Yield**: ~8%, **Expenses**: 0.36 (low), **Beta/Risk**: Low

Strategy – Covered Calls and ELNs with less volatility (downside protection).

What makes JEPI an excellent pick for high monthly retirement income with low risk?

- JEPI is designed to provide high monthly income while maintaining capital appreciation.
- It has a low beta (low risk), has a beta value of 0.5 (S&P 500 beta is 1.0), and pays ~8% annually + tracks growth. JEPI returned a total of 21% in 2021.
- It is a NEW high monthly income product from one of the most respected money managers globally – JP Morgan Chase.
- JEPI targets a significant portion of S&P 500 returns with **less volatility**, seeking annualized income distributed **monthly**.
- It generates income through a combination of selling options and investing in U.S. large-cap stocks.

- It has a low beta value of 0.5, meaning that if the SP500 goes down 1%, JEPI will go down ~0.5%. *Therefore, it is safer than buying even the sp500 index in a market downturn.*
- Its fees are only 0.35%. Very low compared to other similar ETFs.
- It is NEW - not many people know about it yet.
- Given the attributes of low volatility, low risk, low fees, high monthly income – it is a perfect investment for retirees who can enjoy high monthly income on their savings + portfolio growth.
- Follow my instructions in the next chapter, and you should be able to live off the monthly income in retirement - without touching your principal.

#2 Pick: Nationwide Risk Managed Income ETF (NUSI)

Key Facts: **Yield**: 7.82%, **Expenses**: 0.68% (medium)
Beta/Risk: Low (0.44)

Strategy – High Monthly Income Covered Calls with Downside Protection.

What makes NUSI an excellent pick for monthly retirement income with low fees?

- It is less volatile and has downside protection like JEPI.
- It tracks the Nasdaq 100, which is inherently a safe strategy as market indexes always go up over time.
- Its monthly returns are like JEPI, but NUSI's fees are higher and have less growth.
- NUSI tracks the Nasdaq 100 index, which is less safe than JEPI, which tracks the S&P 500 index.
- NUSI contains protective put options that offer downside protection during down markets.
- **In March 2000 pandemic, when the Nasdaq dropped close to 30%, NUSI dropped only 12% and still returned an income of 7.5%+ annually.**

See Figure 19 below on how NUSI performed vs. the Nasdaq index during the March 2020 pandemic market drop. It did not drop as much and continued to generate a high monthly income.

Figure 19: Graph showing NUSI dropping less than the Nasdaq index during the March 2000 pandemic drop while returning 7.5% in income

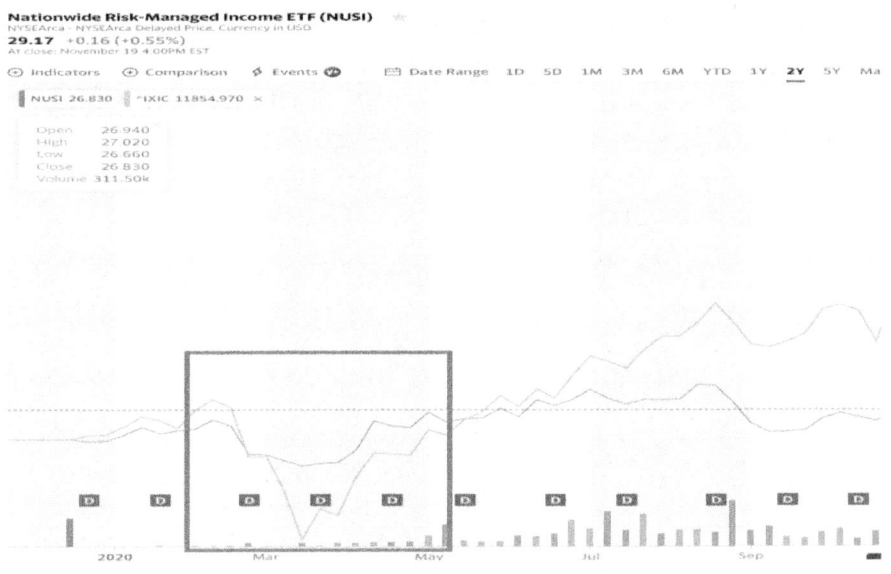

Source: Yahoo Finance (2022)

#3 Pick : Global X Nasdaq 100 Covered Call ETF (QYLD)

Key Facts: **Yield**: ~11%, **Expenses**: 0.60% (medium) **Risk**: Medium/High

Strategy – High Monthly Income Covered Calls (No Downside Protection).

What makes QYLD an excellent pick for monthly retirement income?

- The Global X Nasdaq 100 Covered Call ETF (QYLD) follows a "covered call" or "buy-write" strategy, in which the Fund buys the stocks in the Nasdaq 100 Index and

"writes" or "sells" corresponding call options on the same index.
- It has a very high yield and pays income monthly (~11%) plus growth.
- However, it has no downside protection.
- It performs better in a bull market than JEPI or NUSI, with higher returns. However, it has no downside protection, so it is risky in an overvalued stock market like today.
- The fees are higher than JEPI and about the same as NUSI.

#4 Pick: Russell 2000 Covered Call ETF (RYLD)

Key Facts: Yield: 11.75%, **Expenses:** 0.60% (medium), **Risk:** Medium/High

Strategy – High Monthly Income Covered Calls (No Downside Protection).

What makes RYLD an excellent pick for monthly retirement income?

- RYLD seeks to generate income through covered call writing, which historically produces higher yields in periods of volatility.
- It has the highest yield of the top 4 (~12%) and pays income monthly.
- However, like QYLD, it has no downside protection.
- It performs better in a bull market than JEPI or NUSI. However, it performs worse in an overvalued market (like today) - as it has no downside protection if the market were to drop 50%.

CHAPTER 11
Strategy 1: An Early-Retirement "Set it and Forget it" Strategy.

This high monthly income strategy is the core of the book, where I will show you a simple "set it and forget it" strategy to generate high income with low risk for early retirement.

Let us assume Tom has $500,000 saved in retirement in this example. He wants to generate a high monthly income with low risk without touching the principal - so that he can live worry-free in retirement.

Step 1:

Start with the bucket strategy we discussed earlier. Tom would divide his money into three buckets:

Total: $500,000 in investable assets. Divide the money into three buckets.

Table 11 below shows a simple and safe early retirement strategy for beginners.

Table 11: Safe Early Retirement Strategy for Beginners

Bucket Number	In which year is money used?	Investment Type	Amount	Monthly Income
Bucket 1	Year 1	Cash	$30,000	~$2500 / month
Bucket 2	Year 2	Very Safe fixed income investment (e.g., VMBS, BIV paying 1.35% annually)	$31,000 (~2600/month)	~$2600/month
Bucket 3	Year 3 - rest of life	65% JEPI, 35% NUSI	$440,000 (pays ~8% or ~$3000/month interest) + growth in stock market + downside protection + low fees = never having to touch principal	~3000 / month

> **Important** - Tom should tell his brokerage that he wants dividends paid out in cash (not reinvested). This cash dividend will be moved from bucket 3 to bucket two every year.

In year one:

- Tom would spend cash in Bucket 1.

In year two onwards:

- Tom will move the money from Bucket 2 (~31,000) to Bucket 1.
- Tom will then move cash dividend money from Bucket 3 to Bucket 2 for ~$36,000.

So - every year, Tom will have $36,000 + other income like Social Security, rental income, pension, part-time work to live on – without touching the principal.

Most of the principal is untouched ($440,000 in bucket 3) - only "income earned" is moved from bucket 3 to bucket 2 every year.

The beauty of this approach is that most of your principal is **untouched,** and you still get growth (the underlying index **always** goes up over time).

If the market goes down 40%, you do not need to panic sell. You have the luxury of waiting until it recovers as you are only living off the interest in bucket 3, not the principal.

Plus - JEPI and NUSI have some downside protection built-in - so if the broader market was to drop significantly, JEPI and NUSI should drop much less, making them safer than most other high-income investments.

CHAPTER 12
Strategy 2: An Active Strategy for Even Higher Returns

How is the active strategy different than the passive strategy?

The active strategy is like the passive strategy in several ways. First, it follows the bucket strategy where we have cash in Bucket 1, safe income funds in Bucket 2, and high yield monthly income funds in Bucket 3.

However, the difference is the funds you buy in Bucket 3.

In the active strategy, you need to determine if you are in an undervalued or overvalued stock market cycle.

If you are in an overvalued market cycle like today, in Bucket 3, you invest 65% in JEPI and 35% in NUSI (like the passive strategy).

However, if you are in an **undervalued** stock market, in Bucket 3, you invest 50% in RYLD and 50% in QYLD for **even** higher returns (11%+). Remember, the passive strategy is paying you about ~8%.

Bottom line – you can optimize your investments depending on the type of market you are in. I will also give you free notifications on my website, "retirementmonthlyincome.com," when we move from overvalued to undervalued markets or vice versa.

To summarize, if we are in an overvalued market like today, I invest in high-monthly-income ETFs with downside protection (JEPI, NUSI).

However, if we are in an undervalued market, I invest in even higher-yielding covered call ETFs for an additional performance boost (QYLD, RYLD).

However, I suggest most novice investors start with the passive strategy, as it is simpler to understand and implement.

How will I know if we are in an undervalued or overvalued stock market?

Several data points tell us if we are in an overvalued, neutral, or undervalued stock market.

One metric is the sp500 mean reversion.

"Mean reversion" refers to the financial concept that a stock's price (or an index like the S&P 500), over the long-term, will always fluctuate around its mean. Therefore, if the market had a positive/negative change to its actual returns, mean reversion would cause a negative/positive change.

As you might have guessed, the stock is considered undervalued when the current stock price is less than this historical average price. On the other hand, the stock is considered overvalued when the current stock price is above the historical average price.

The S&P 500 Reversion chart shown in Figure 20 can be graphed using inflation-adjusted S&P 500 returns and an exponential regression trend line, as shown below from 1970 - 2021:

Figure 20: Graph showing why I think the stock market is due for a significant correction

Source: https://www.currentmarketvaluation.com/models/s&p500-mean-reversion.php

In addition, you can subscribe to my free newsletter at retirementmonthlyincome.com, where I send out monthly updates as to whether we are in an undervalued, overvalued, or neutral market based on several data points.

Below is a summary of the active strategy:

Table 12 below is a summary of the active strategy for more sophisticated investors for higher returns:

Table 12: An Active Strategy for Higher Returns than the Passive Strategy

Assume $500,000 retirement savings.

Strategy	Market Type	Bucket 1 (Year 1)	Bucket 2 (Year 2)	Bucket 3 (Year 3+)	Projected Monthly Income
Passive (recommended for newer investors)	Doesn't matter	Cash ($30,000)	Safe Bonds ($31,000)	Safe Covered Call ETF's (65% JEPI, 35% NUSI)	$440,000 at 8% = $3000/month + growth + not touching principal
Active (recommended for sophisticated investors)	Undervalued Stock Market	Cash ($30,000)	Safe Bonds ($31,000)	Covered Call ETF's (50% RYLD, 50% QYLD)	$440,000 at 11% = $4030/month + growth + not touching principal
Active (recommended for sophisticated investors)	Overvalued Stock Market (basically the same as passive)	Cash ($30,000)	Safe Bonds ($31,000)	Safe Covered Call ETF's (65% JEPI, 35% NUSI)	$440,000 at 8% = $3000/month + growth + not touching principal

CHAPTER 13
Conclusion + BONUS

As a retiree, it is tough to generate high monthly income with low risk given market conditions today. The stock market is overvalued, and interest rates are low, making generating high returns risky and complex.

In addition, there is strong evidence that the recommended retirement investment strategy of 60% stocks to 40% bonds will have low returns for the foreseeable future.

There are many high monthly income investments available today, but unfortunately, as I have shown, most are high risk.

As a financial veteran specializing in algorithmic trading and fixed income models, I have tested hundreds of strategies in bull and bear markets to find investments that generate high monthly income with low risk. Unfortunately, there are very few investments that make the cut.

I found that the best strategy to generate high monthly income with low risk is investing in covered calls. Covered calls were once very complex and reserved for a few sophisticated traders; however, it is as easy as buying a stock with new investments that have come to the market.

When selecting investments for high retirement income, the key metrics to watch out for are "beta" and "yield," which give you the risk and income of an investment.

Beta shows you the volatility or risk of an investment. Typically, the more volatile an investment, the riskier it is. For example, the S&P 500 index has a Beta of 1, while our #1 pick JEPI has 0.5.

Yield is a measure of income provided by your investment. The key here is to look for high-income (high yield) investments, paying monthly with low risk (low beta).

My #1 pick JEPI, has a yield of ~8% + low Beta + growth as it tracks the S&P 500.

The S&P 500 index (and thereby JEPI) will *always go up over time*, even if there are short-term dips and downturns.

In terms of risk: buying an individual stock is riskier than buying a basket of stocks Likewise, buying a specific sector (like real estate) is riskier than buying the S&P 500 index.

As a retiree, I would stay away from buying individual stocks or specific sectors - as they are inherently riskier.

For example, during the crisis of 2008, the financial and real estate sectors were hit particularly hard. During the March 2020 pandemic, real estate sectors lost 40% of their value in less than two months.

Therefore, investing in a broader index is inherently safer. The sp500 index, DOW, and Nasdaq will *always* go up over time. So, you will not be tempted to panic sell if there is a significant downturn in the markets.

The strategy here is that your money is divided into three buckets

Bucket 1: Cash for one year

Bucket 2: Safe Bonds for 1-2 years

Bucket 3: JEPI/NUSI or RYLD/QYLD – High monthly, low-risk investments for your largest bucket. In case of a prolonged market downturn, you will still get a high monthly income (to move to other buckets), and eventually, the indexes (SP500,

Nasdaq) will turn as they always go up over time, which will grow the value of this bucket to last a lifetime.

In case of a prolonged market downturn, you will still get a high monthly income (to move to other buckets), and eventually, the indexes (SP500, Nasdaq) will turn as they always go up over time.

You should be able to live off the high monthly income and leave your principal untouched in bucket 3.

Again, my top 4 covered call ETFs for high monthly income with low risk are JEPI, NUSI, RYLD, and QYLD in that order. Again, I have shown you the data behind the "why" and shown how they have performed in both up and down markets.

I have 65% of my 3rd bucket in JEPI and 35% NUSI in my 3rd bucket and live off the 8% dividends without touching my principal for my passive portfolio. On a $500,000 nest egg, I can generate at least $3000/month in income without touching my principal and receive automatic downside protection + growth over the years: all with low fees.

I assess if I am in an overvalued or an undervalued stock market based on multiple indicators for my active portfolio.

In an overvalued stock market (like today), I use the same passive strategy of 65% JEPI and 35% NUSI.

In an undervalued stock market, I will invest 50% in RYLD and 50% QYLD in my third bucket and live off the 11% dividend income without touching my principal.

On a $500,000 nest egg, I will be able to generate $4030/month in income without touching my principal + with downside protection + growth over the years.

Recap:

Table 13 below shows a recap of how the passive and active strategies are Implemented for maximum monthly income with low risk.

Table 13: Recap of the Key Active and Passive Strategies

Assume $500,000 retirement savings.

Strategy	Market Type	Bucket 1 (Year 1)	Bucket 2 (Year 2)	Bucket 3 (Year 3+)	Projected Monthly Income
Passive	Doesn't matter	Cash ($30,000)	Safe Bonds ($31,000)	Safe Covered Call ETF's (65% JEPI, 35% NUSI)	$440,000 at 8% = ~$3000/month + growth + not touching principal
Active	Undervalued Stock Market (*stock market at lows*)	Cash ($30,000)	Safe Bonds ($31,000)	Covered Call ETF's (50% RYLD, 50% QYLD)	$440,000 at 11% = $4030/month + growth + not touching principal
Active	Overvalued Stock Market (*stock market at highs*)	Cash ($30,000)	Safe Bonds ($31,000)	Safe Covered Call ETF's (65% JEPI, 35% NUSI)	$440,000 at 8% = $3000/month + growth + not touching principal

BONUS

There is much information here to digest, and you may want to speak to a financial advisor to answer questions and have them create a personalized high monthly income plan for you.

I am connected to a network of "vetted" financial advisors specializing in high monthly income covered call strategies – similar to what is discussed in this book.

As a bonus and thank you for purchasing my book, I will connect you to one of my vetted financial advisors for a free 30 min session. The advisor will review your situation and create a personalized monthly income plan for you (using similar strategies have outlined in the book), plus answer any questions you may have.

I suggest starting with a short conversation with a financial advisor to answer any questions you may have.

To get started:

Go to "retirementmonthlyincome.com" and enter your information in the "consult with an advisor" section.

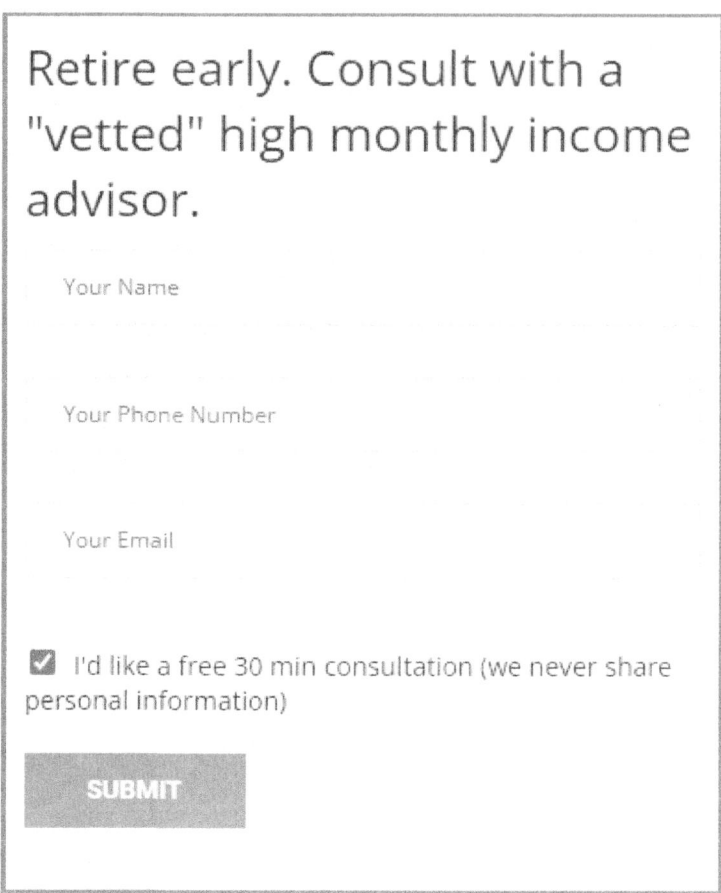

Also - Mimic my trading strategies for free:

Subscribe to my free newsletter at retirementmonthlyincome.com. I provide a monthly newsletter informing you of the market cycle we are in and whether I am following a safe passive high monthly income path or a more active path for higher income.

I recommend starting with the passive set-it-and-forget-it strategy outlined in the book to keep things simple as a new investor.

The investment strategies I have shown are ones I use in my portfolio. After testing hundreds of strategies through bull and bear markets in several assets classes, I have discovered "what works."

Covered calls mainly were overlooked as a retirement vehicle due to their complexity, but with new investments that have come to market – they are very effective for generating high monthly income with low risk, and it is now as easy as buying a stock.

I no longer worry much about the stock market's daily gyrations and get repeatable high monthly income with low risk - so I can live financially stress-free.

Again, thank you for reading; I hope you found this book helpful, and I hope you can apply the strategies I have outlined in the book.

Please feel free to reach out to me directly at info@retirementmonthlyincom.com for any questions or comments you may have. I respond to ALL messages. I look forward to hearing from you and helping you on your path to a financially secure retirement!

WHAT DID YOU THINK OF "HOW TO RETIRE EARLY"?

First, thank you for purchasing my book "How to retire early". I know you could have picked any number of books to read, but you picked this book and for that I am extremely grateful.

I hope that it added at value and quality to your everyday life. If so, it would be great if you could share this book with your friends and family.

If you enjoyed this book and found some benefit in reading this, I'd like to hear from you and hope that you could take some time to post a review on Amazon. Your feedback and support will help this author to greatly improve his writing craft for future projects and make this book even better.

You can follow this link here.

I want you, the reader, to know that your review is very important and so, if you'd like to leave a review, all you have to do is click here and away you go. I wish you all the best for a happy and fulfilling retirement!

Printed in Great Britain
by Amazon